BEST-LOVED
POEMS

BEST-LOVED POEMS

EDITED BY PATRICIA A. PINGRY

IDEALS PUBLICATIONS
NASHVILLE, TENNESSEE

EDITOR'S NOTE

On the following pages are more than two hundred wonderful poems, some dating to Shakespeare's time, others from the present generation of poets. The poems were selected based on surveys from readers of *Ideals* magazine who submitted some of their favorite poems. Additional selections are those classic poems that have stood the test of time. Without exception, the poems are from English-language poets, since we believe that poetry is best read in its native language.

To achieve some form to the book, we felt it necessary to categorize the selections, recognizing at the same time that good poetry defies categorization and speaks differently to every reader.

William Wordsworth called poetry "wisdom married to immortal verse." We hope that *Best-Loved Poems* offers some wisdom to its readers, along with familiar, sometimes magnificent, sometimes humble, but always "immortal" verse.

Library of Congress Cataloging-in-Publication Data
The Ideals treasury of best loved poems / edited by Patricia A.
Pingry. — 1st ed.
  p. cm.
  Includes index.
  ISBN 0-8249-4128-4
  1. English poetry. 2. American Poetry. I. Pingry, Patricia A.
PR1175.I28   1997
821.008—DC21   97-18918
                                                         CIP

Publisher and Editor, Patricia A. Pingry
Associate Editor, Michelle Prater Burke
Book Designer, Tina Wells Davenport
Editorial Assistant, Tara E. Lynn
Editorial Intern, Melissa A. Chronister

Artwork by Stacy Venturi Pickett and Leslie Sheets

Printed and bound in Italy.
Color film separations by Precision Color Graphics,
Franklin, Wisconsin

Published by Ideals Publications, a Guideposts Company
535 Metroplex Drive, Suite 250
Nashville, Tennessee 37211
www.idealsbooks.com

10 9 8 7 6 5 4 3

ACKNOWLEDGMENTS

Ideals Publications has made every effort to trace the ownership of all copyrighted material. Thanks are due to the following authors, publishers, and agents for permission to use the material indicated:

Frost, Robert, "Mending Wall," "Moon Compasses," "Mowing," "A Prayer in Spring," "Reluctance," "Stopping by Woods on a Snowy Evening," and "The Road Not Taken." From *The Poetry of Robert Frost* edited by Edward Connery Lathem. Copyright © 1923, 1930, 1934, 1939, 1969 by Henry Holt and Co.; copyright © 1944, 1951, 1958, 1962 by Robert Frost; © 1967 by Lesley Frost Ballantine. Reprinted by permission of Henry Holt & Co., Inc.
Guest, Edgar A., "Home," "It Couldn't Be Done," "Just Folks," "Let's Be Brave," and "Sittin' on the Porch." Reprinted by permission of the author's estate.
Guiterman, Arthur, "A Little Lost Pup." From *The Laughing Muse* by Arthur Guiterman. Reprinted by permission of Louise H. Sclove.
Housman, A. E., "When I Was One-and-Twenty." Reprinted with permission of The Society of Authors as the literary representative of the Estate of A. E. Housman.
Hughes, Langston, "Dream Variation." Copyright © 1926 by Alfred A. Knopf, Inc., renewed 1954 by Langston Hughes.
Malloch, Douglas, "Up and Doing." Reprinted by permission of the author's estate.
Masefield, John, "Sea Fever." Reprinted with permission of The Society of

Authors as the literary representative of the Estate of John Masefield.
Moore, Rosalie, "Catalogue." Reprinted by permission; © 1940 The New Yorker Magazine, Inc. All rights reserved.
Nash, Ogden, "The Tale of Custard the Dragon." Copyright © 1945 by Ogden Nash, renewed. Reprinted by permission of Curtis Brown, Ltd. and Little, Brown & Company.
Robinson, Corinne Roosevelt, "The Path That Leads to Nowhere." Reprinted with the permission of Scribner, a Division of Simon & Schuster from *The Poems of Corinne Roosevelt Robinson*. Copyright © 1921 by Charles Scribner's Sons, renewed 1949 by Corinne R. Alsop.
Roethke, Theodore, "The Waking." Copyright © 1953 by Theodore Roethke. From *The Collected Poems of Theodore Roethke* by Theodore Roethke. Used by permission of Doubleday, a division of Bantam Doubleday Dell Publishing Group, Inc.
Sandburg, Carl, "Fog." From *Chicago Poems* by Carl Sandburg, copyright © 1916 by Holt, Rinehart and Winston, Inc. and renewed 1944 by Carl Sandburg, reprinted by permission of Harcourt Brace & Company.
Teasdale, Sara, "Barter." Reprinted with the permission of Simon & Schuster from *Collected Poems of Sara Teasdale*. Copyright © 1917 by Macmillan Publishing Company, renewed 1945 by Mamie T. Wheless.
Thomas, Dylan, "Do Not Go Gentle into That Good Night." From *The Poems of Dylan Thomas*. Copyright © 1925 by Dylan Thomas. Reprinted by permission of New Directions Publishing Corporation and David Higham Associates.

TABLE OF CONTENTS

Nature

GOD'S WORLD
EDNA ST. VINCENT MILLAY

O world, I cannot hold thee close enough!
  Thy winds, thy wide grey skies!
  Thy mists, that roll and rise!
Thy woods, this autumn day, that ache and sag
And all but cry with colour! That gaunt crag
To crush! To lift the lean of that black bluff!
World, World, I cannot get thee close enough!

Poems

Long have I known a glory in it all,
   But never knew I this:
   Here such a passion is
As stretcheth me apart,—Lord, I do fear
Thou'st made the world too beautiful this year;

My soul is all but out of me,—let fall
No burning leaf; prithee, let no bird call.

BARTER
SARA TEASDALE

Life has loveliness to sell,
   All beautiful and splendid things,
Blue waves whitened on a cliff,
   Soaring fire that sways and sings,
And children's faces looking up
Holding wonder like a cup.

Life has loveliness to sell,
   Music like a curve of gold,
Scent of pine trees in the rain,

Eyes that love you, arms that hold,
And for your spirit's still delight,
Holy thoughts that star the night.

Spend all you have for loveliness,
   Buy it and never count the cost;
For one white singing hour of peace
   Count many a year of strife well lost,
And for a breath of ecstasy
Give all you have been, or could be.

PIED BEAUTY
GERARD MANLEY HOPKINS

Glory be to God for dappled things—
      For skies of couple-colour as a brinded cow;
      For rose-moles all in stipple upon trout that swim;

Fresh-fire-coal chestnut-falls; finches' wings;
      Landscape plotted and pieced—fold, fallow, and plough;
         And all trades, their gear and tackle and trim.

All things counter, original, spare, strange;
      Whatever is fickle, freckled (who knows how?)
         With swift, slow; sweet, sour; adazzle, dim;
He fathers-forth whose beauty is past change:
         Praise him.

A PRAYER IN SPRING
ROBERT FROST

Oh, give us pleasure in the flowers today;
And give us not to think so far away
As the uncertain harvest; keep us here
All simply in the springing of the year.

Oh, give us pleasure in the orchard white,
Like nothing else by day, like ghosts by night;
And make us happy in the happy bees,
The swarm dilating round the perfect trees.

And make us happy in the darting bird
That suddenly above the bees is heard,
The meteor that thrusts in with needle bill,
And off a blossom in mid air stands still.

For this is love and nothing else is love,
The which it is reserved for God above
To sanctify to what far ends He will,
But which it only needs that we fulfill.

There Was a Roaring in the Wind All Night
William Wordsworth

There was a roaring in the wind all night;
The rain came heavily and fell in floods;
But now the sun is rising calm and bright;
The birds are singing in the distant woods;
Over his own sweet voice the Stock-dove broods;
The Jay makes answer as the Magpie chatters;
And all the air is filled with pleasant noise of waters.

All things that love the sun are out of doors;
The sky rejoices in the morning's birth;
The grass is bright with rain-drops;—on the moors
The hare is running races in her mirth;
And with her feet she from the plashy earth
Raises a mist, that, glittering in the sun,
Runs with her all the way, wherever she doth run.

Rain Song
Robert Loveman

It isn't raining for me,
　　It's raining daffodils;
In every dimpled drop I see
　　Wild flowers on the hills.
The clouds of gray engulf the day
　　And overwhelm the town;
It isn't raining rain to me,
　　It's raining roses down.

It isn't raining rain to me,
　　But fields of clover bloom,
Where any buccaneering bee
　　Can find a bed and room.
A health unto the happy,
　　A fig for him who frets!
It isn't raining rain to me,
　　It's raining violets.

It's raining violets

A Light Exists in Spring
Emily Dickinson

A Light exists in Spring
Not present on the Year
At any other period—
When March is scarcely here

A Color stands abroad
On Solitary Fields
That Science cannot overtake
But Human Nature feels.

It waits upon the Lawn,
It shows the furthest Tree
Upon the furthest Slope you know
It almost speaks to you.

Then as Horizons step
Or Noons report away
Without the Formula of sound
It passes and we stay—

A quality of loss
Affecting our Content
As Trade had suddenly encroached
Upon a Sacrament.

FROM Pippa Passes
Robert Browning

The year's at the spring
And day's at the morn;
Morning's at seven;

The hillside's dew-pearled;
The lark's on the wing;
The snail's on the thorn:
God's in his heaven—
All's right with the world!

My Heart Leaps Up
William Wordsworth

My heart leaps up when I behold
    A rainbow in the sky:
So was it when my life began;
So is it now I am a man;
So be it when I shall grow old,
    Or let me die!
The Child is father of the Man;
And I could wish my days to be
Bound each to each by natural piety.

MENDING WALL
ROBERT FROST

Something there is that doesn't love a wall,
That sends the frozen-ground-swell under it
And spills the upper boulders in the sun,
And makes gaps even two can pass abreast.
The work of hunters is another thing:
I have come after them and made repair
Where they have left not one stone on a stone,
But they would have the rabbit out of hiding,
To please the yelping dogs. The gaps I mean,
No one has seen them made or heard them made,
But at spring mending-time we find them there.
I let my neighbor know beyond the hill;
And on a day we meet to walk the line
And set the wall between us once again.
We keep the wall between us as we go.
To each the boulders that have fallen to each.
And some are loaves and some so nearly balls
We have to use a spell to make them balance:
'Stay where you are until our backs are turned!'
We wear our fingers rough with handling them.
Oh, just another kind of outdoor game,

One on a side. It comes to little more:
There where it is we do not need the wall:
He is all pine and I am apple orchard.
My apple trees will never get across
And eat the cones under his pines, I tell him.
He only says, 'Good fences make good neighbors.'
Spring is the mischief in me, and I wonder
If I could put a notion in his head:
'Why do they make good neighbors? Isn't it
Where there are cows? But here there are no cows.
Before I built a wall I'd ask to know
What I was walling in or walling out,
And to whom I was like to give offense.
Something there is that doesn't love a wall,
That wants it down.' I could say 'Elves' to him,
But it's not elves exactly, and I'd rather
He said it for himself. I see him there,
Bringing a stone grasped firmly by the top
In each hand, like an old-stone savage armed.
He moves in darkness as it seems to me,
Not of woods only and the shade of trees.
He will not go behind his father's saying,
And he likes having thought of it so well
He says again, 'Good fences make good neighbors.'

A Bird Came Down the Walk
EMILY DICKINSON

A Bird came down the Walk—
He did not know I saw—
He bit an Angleworm in halves
And ate the fellow, raw,

And then he drank a Dew
From a convenient Grass—
And then hopped sidewise to the Wall
To let a Beetle pass—

He glanced with rapid eyes
That hurried all around—

They looked like frightened Beads, I thought—
He stirred his Velvet Head

Like one in danger, Cautious,
I offered him a Crumb
And he unrolled his feathers
And rowed him softer home—

Than Oars divide the Ocean,
Too silver for a seam—
Or Butterflies, off Banks of Noon
Leap, plashless as they swim.

Did You Ever Hear an English Sparrow Sing?
BERTHA JOHNSTON

What? an English sparrow sing?
    Insignificant brown thing,
So common and so bold, 'twould surely bring
    Tears of laughter to the eyes
    Of the superficial wise
To suggest that that small immigrant could sing.

    'Twas the bleakest wintry day,
    Earth, sky, water, all were gray,
Of the universe old Boreas seemed king,
    As he swept across the lake,
    But his empire was at stake,
When that little English sparrow dared to sing.

    Not a friend on earth had I,
    No horizon to my sky,
No faith that there could be another spring.
    Cold the world as that gray wall
    Of the Auditorium tall
Where I heard that little English sparrow sing.

Hark, Hark, the Lark
FROM Cymbeline
WILLIAM SHAKESPEARE

Hark, hark! the lark at heaven's gate sings,
    And Phoebus 'gins arise,
His steeds to water at those springs
    On chalic'd flowers that lies;
And winking Mary-buds begin
    To ope their golden eyes.
With every thing that pretty is,
    My lady sweet, arise:
        Arise, arise!

The Eagle
ALFRED, LORD TENNYSON

He clasps the crag with crooked hands;
Close to the sun in lonely lands,
Ring'd with the azure world, he stands.

The wrinkled sea beneath him crawls;
He watches from his mountain walls,
And like a thunderbolt he falls.

OH, THE WILD JOY OF LIVING
Robert Browning

Oh, the wild joy of living! the leaping from rock up to rock,
The strong rending of boughs from the fir-tree, the cool silver shock
Of the plunge in the pool's living water, the hunt of the bear,
And the sultriness showing the lion couched in his lair.
And the meal, the rich dates yellowed over the gold dust divine,
And the locust-flesh steeped in the pitcher, the full draft of wine,
And the sleep in the dried river-channel where bulrushes tell
That the water was wont to go marbling so softly and well.
How good is man's life, the mere living! how fit to employ
All the heart and the soul and the senses forever in joy!

DAFFODILS
William Wordsworth

I wandered lonely as a cloud
That floats on high o'er vales and hills,
When all at once I saw a crowd,—
A host, of golden daffodils,
Beside the lake, beneath the trees,
Fluttering and dancing in the breeze.

Continuous as the stars that shine
And twinkle on the Milky Way,
They stretched in never-ending line
Along the margin of a bay:
Ten thousand saw I at a glance,
Tossing their heads in sprightly dance.

The waves beside them danced; but they
Outdid the sparkling waves in glee:
A poet could not but be gay,
In such a jocund company!
I gazed—and gazed—but little thought
What wealth the show to me had brought:

For oft, when on my couch I lie
In vacant or in pensive mood,
They flash upon that inward eye
Which is the bliss of solitude;
And then my heart with pleasure fills,
And dances with the daffodils.

A host of golden daffodils . . .

BIRCHES
ROBERT FROST

When I see birches bend to left and right
Across the lines of straighter darker trees,
I like to think some boy's been swinging them.
But swinging doesn't bend them down to stay.
Ice-storms do that. Often you must have seen them
Loaded with ice a sunny winter morning
After a rain. They click upon themselves
As the breeze rises, and turn many-colored
As the stir cracks and crazes their enamel.
Soon the sun's warmth makes them shed crystal shells
Shattering and avalanching on the snow-crust—
Such heaps of broken glass to sweep away
You'd think the inner dome of heaven had fallen.
They are dragged to the withered bracken by the load,
And they seem not to break; though once they are bowed
So low for long, they never right themselves:
You may see their trunks arching in the woods
Years afterwards, trailing their leaves on the ground
Like girls on hands and knees that throw their hair
Before them over their heads to dry in the sun.
But I was going to say when Truth broke in
With all her matter-of-fact about the ice-storm

(Now am I free to be poetical?)
I should prefer to have some boy bend them
As he went out and in to fetch the cows—
Some boy too far from town to learn baseball,
Whose only play was what he found himself,
Summer or winter, and could play alone.
One by one he subdued his father's trees
By riding them down over and over again
Until he took the stiffness out of them,
And not one but hung limp, not one was left
For him to conquer. He learned all there was
To learn about not launching out too soon
And so not carrying the tree away
Clear to the ground. He always kept his poise
To the top branches, climbing carefully
With the same pains you use to fill a cup
Up to the brim, and even above the brim.
Then he flung outward, feet first, with a swish,
Kicking his way down through the air to the ground.
So I was once myself a swinger of birches.
And so I dream of going back to be.
It's when I'm weary of considerations,
And life is too much like a pathless wood
Where your face burns and tickles with the cobwebs
Broken across it, and one eye is weeping
From a twig's having lashed across it open.
I'd like to get away from earth awhile
And then come back to it and begin over.
May no fate wilfully misunderstand me
And half grant what I wish and snatch me away
Not to return. Earth's the right place for love:
I don't know where it's likely to go better.
I'd like to go by climbing a birch tree,
And climb black branches up a snow-white trunk
Toward heaven, till the tree could bear no more,
But dipped its top and set me down again.
That would be good both going and coming back.
One could do worse than be a swinger of birches.

To the Virgins to Make Much of Time
ROBERT HERRICK

Gather ye rosebuds while ye may,
   Old Time is still a-flying;
And this same flower that smiles today,
   Tomorrow will be dying.

The glorious lamp of heaven, the sun,
   The higher he's a-getting,
The sooner will his race be run,
   And nearer he's to setting.

That age is best which is the first,
   When youth and blood are warmer;
But being spent, the worse and worst
   Times still succeed the former.

Then be not coy, but use your time,
   And while ye may, go marry;
For, having lost but once your prime,
   You may forever tarry.

The Road Not Taken
ROBERT FROST

Two roads diverged in a yellow wood,
And sorry I could not travel both
And be one traveler, long I stood
And looked down one as far as I could
To where it bent in the undergrowth;

Then took the other, as just as fair,
And having perhaps the better claim,
Because it was grassy and wanted wear;
Though as for that the passing there
Had worn them really about the same.

And both that morning equally lay
In leaves no step had trodden black.
Oh, I kept the first for another day!
Yet knowing how way leads on to way,
I doubted if I should ever come back.

I shall be telling this with a sigh
Somewhere ages and ages hence:
Two roads diverged in a wood, and I—
I took the one less traveled by,
And that has made all the difference.

A Thing of Beauty Is a Joy Forever
JOHN KEATS

A thing of beauty is a joy forever:
Its loveliness increases; it will never
Pass into nothingness; but still will keep
A bower quiet for us, and a sleep
Full of sweet dreams, and health, and quiet breathing.
Therefore, on every morrow, are we wreathing
A flowery band to bind us to the earth,
Spite of despondence, of the human dearth
Of noble natures, of the gloomy days,
Of all the unhealthy and o'er-darken'd ways
Made for our searching: yes, in spite of all,
Some shape of beauty moves away the pall
From our dark spirits. Such the sun, the moon,
Trees old and young, sprouting a shady boon
For simple sheep; and such are daffodils
With the green world they live in and clear rills
That for themselves a cooling covert make
'Gainst the hot season; the mid-forest brake,
Rich with a sprinkling of fair musk-rose blooms:
And such too is the grandeur of the dooms
We have imagined for the mighty dead;
All lovely tales that we have heard or read:
An endless fountain of immortal drink,
Pouring unto us from the heaven's brink.

The Chambered Nautilus
Oliver Wendell Holmes

This is the ship of pearl, which, poets feign,
    Sails the unshadowed main,—
    The venturous bark that flings
On the sweet summer wind its purpled wings
In gulfs enchanted, where the Siren sings,
    And coral reefs lie bare,
Where the cold sea-maids rise to sun their streaming hair.

Its webs of living gauze no more unfurl;
    Wrecked is the ship of pearl!
    And every chambered cell,
Where its dim dreaming life was wont to dwell,
As the frail tenant shaped his growing shell,
    Before thee lies revealed,—
Its irised ceiling rent, its sunless crypt unsealed!

Year after year beheld the silent toil
    That spread his lustrous coil;
    Still, as the spiral grew,
He left the past year's dwelling for the new,
Stole with soft step its shining archway through,
    Built up its idle door,
Stretched in his last-found home, and knew the old no more.

Thanks for the heavenly message brought by thee,
    Child of the wandering sea,
    Cast from her lap, forlorn!
From thy dead lips a clearer note is born
Than ever Triton blew from wreathèd horn!
    While on mine ear it rings,
Through the deep caves of thought I hear a voice that sings:—

Build thee more stately mansions, O my soul,
    As the swift seasons roll!
    Leave thy low-vaulted past!
Let each new temple, nobler than the last,
Shut thee from heaven with a dome more vast,
    Till thou at length art free,
Leaving thine outgrown shell by life's unresting sea!

from Green River
William Cullen Bryant

    When breezes are soft and skies are fair,
I steal an hour from study and care,
And hie me away to the woodland scene,
Where wanders the stream with waters of green,
As if the bright fringe of herbs on its brink
Had given their stain to the waves they drink;
And they, whose meadows it murmurs through,
Have named the stream from its own fair hue.

    Yet pure its waters—its shallows are bright
With colored pebbles and sparkles of light,
And clear the depths where its eddies play,
And dimples deepen and whirl away,
And the plane-tree's speckled arms o'ershoot
The swifter current that mines its root,
Through whose shifting leaves, as you walk the hill,
The quivering glimmer of sun and rill
With a sudden flash on the eye is thrown,
Like the ray that streams from the diamond-stone.
Oh, loveliest there the spring days come,
With blossoms, and birds, and wild-bees' hum;
The flowers of summer are fairest there,
And freshest the breath of the summer air;
And sweetest the golden autumn day
In silence and sunshine glides away.

ADDRESS TO THE OCEAN
FROM CHILDE HAROLD'S PILGRIMAGE
George Gordon, Lord Byron

Roll on, thou deep and dark blue Ocean—roll!
Ten thousand fleets sweep over thee in vain:
Man marks the earth with ruin—his control
Stops with the shore;—upon the watery plain
The wrecks are all thy deed, nor doth remain
A shadow of man's ravage, save his own,
When for a moment, like a drop of rain,
He sinks into thy depths with bubbling groan,
Without a grave, unknell'd, uncoffin'd and unknown.

His steps are not upon thy paths—thy fields
Are not a spoil for him—thou dost arise
And shake him from thee; the vile strength he wields
For earth's destruction thou dost all despise,
Spurning him from thy bosom to the skies,
And send'st him, shivering in thy playful spray,
And howling, to his Gods, where haply lies
His petty hope in some near port or bay,
And dashest him again to earth—there let him lay.

The armaments which thunderstrike the walls
Of rock-built cities, bidding nations quake,
And monarchs tremble in their capitals,
The oak leviathans, whose huge ribs make
Their clay creator the vain title take

Of lord of thee, and arbiter of war—
These are thy toys, and, as the snowy flake,
They melt into thy yeast of waves, which mar
Alike the Armada's pride, or spoils of Trafalgar.

Thou glorious mirror, where the Almighty's form
Glasses itself in tempests: in all time,
Calm or convulsed—in breeze, or gale, or storm,
Icing the pole, or in the torrid clime
Dark-heaving;—boundless, endless, and sublime—
The image of Eternity—the throne
Of the Invisible; even from out thy slime
The monsters of the deep are made; each zone
Obeys thee; thou goest forth, dread, fathomless, alone.

And I have loved thee, Ocean! and my joy
Of youthful sports was on thy breast to be
Borne, like thy bubbles, onward: from a boy
I wanton'd with thy breakers—they to me
Were a delight; and if the freshening sea
Made them a terror—'twas a pleasing fear,
For I was as it were a child of thee,
And trusted to thy billows far and near,
And laid my hand upon thy mane—as I do here.

THE SOUND OF THE SEA
Henry Wadsworth Longfellow

The sea awoke at midnight from its sleep,
And round the pebbly beaches far and wide
I heard the first wave of the rising tide
Rush onward with uninterrupted sweep;
A voice out of the silence of the deep,
A sound mysteriously multiplied
As of a cataract from the mountain's side,

Or roar of winds upon a wooded steep.
So comes to us at times, from the unknown
And inaccessible solitudes of being,
The rushing of the sea-tides of the soul;
And inspirations, that we deem our own,
Are some divine foreshadowing and foreseeing
Of things beyond our reason or control.

NATURE
HENRY WADSWORTH LONGFELLOW

As a fond mother, when the day is o'er,
    Leads by the hand her little child to bed,
    Half willing, half reluctant to be led,
    And leaves his broken playthings
        on the floor,
Still gazing at them through the open door,
    Nor wholly reassured and comforted
    By promises of others in their stead,
    Which, though more splendid,
        may not please him more;
So Nature deals with us, and takes away
    Our playthings one by one,
        and by the hand
    Leads us to rest so gently, that we go
Scarce knowing if we wish to go or stay,
    Being too full of sleep to understand
    How far the unknown transcends
        the what we know.

FLOWER IN THE CRANNIED WALL
ALFRED, LORD TENNYSON

Flower in the crannied wall,
I pluck you out of the crannies,
I hold you here, root and all, in my hand,
Little flower—but *if* I could understand
What you are, root and all, and all in all,
I should know what God and man is.

THE MOUNTAINS ARE A LONELY FOLK
HAMLIN GARLAND

The mountains they are silent folk,
    They stand afar—alone;
And the clouds that kiss their brows at night
    Hear neither sign nor groan.
    Each bears him in his ordered place
    As soldiers do, and bold and high
They fold their forests round their feet
    And bolster up the sky.

OUT IN THE FIELDS
AUTHOR UNKNOWN

The little cares that fretted me,
    I lost them yesterday
Among the fields above the sea,
    Among the winds that play,
Among the lowing of the herds,
    The rustling of the trees,
Among the singing of the birds,
    The humming of the bees.

The foolish fears of what might pass,
    I cast them all away
Among the clover-scented grass,
    Among the new-mown hay,
Among the hushing of the corn,
    Where drowsy poppies nod,
Where ill thoughts die and good are born—
    Out in the fields of God.

NIGHT
WILLIAM BLAKE

The sun descending in the west,
  The evening star does shine;
The birds are silent in their nest.
  And I must seek for mine.
    The moon, like a flower
    In heaven's high bower,
    With silent delight
    Sits and smiles on the night.

Farewell, green fields and happy grove,
  Where flocks have took delight:
Where lambs have nibbled, silent move
  The feet of angels bright;
    Unseen they pour blessing
    And joy without ceasing
    On each bud and blossom
    On each sleeping bosom.

And there the lion's ruddy eyes
  Shall flow with tears of gold:
And pitying the tender cries,
  And walking round the fold:
    Saying, "Wrath by His meekness,
    And, by His health, sickness,
    Are driven away
    From our immortal day.

"And now beside thee, bleating lamb,
  I can lie down and sleep,
Or think on Him who bore thy name,
  Graze after thee, and weep.
    For, wash'd in life's river,
    My bright mane for ever
    Shall shine like the gold
    As I guard o'er the fold."

DAYBREAK
HENRY WADSWORTH LONGFELLOW

A Wind came up out of the sea,
And said, "O mists, make room for me."

It hailed the ships, and cried, "Sail on,
Ye mariners, the night is gone."

And hurried landward far away,
Crying, "Awake! it is the day."

It said unto the forest, "Shout!
Hang all your leafy banners out!"

It touched the wood-bird's folded wing,
And said, "O bird, awake and sing."

And o'er the farms, "O chanticleer,
Your clarion blow; the day is near."

It whispered to the fields of corn,
"Bow down, and hail the coming morn."

It shouted through the belfry-tower,
"Awake, O bell! proclaim the hours."

It crossed the churchyard with a sigh,
And said, "Not yet! in quiet lie."

. . . their brows at night

SUNRISE AND SUNSET
EMILY DICKINSON

I'll tell you how the sun rose,—
A ribbon at a time.
The steeples swam in amethyst,
The news like squirrels ran.

The hills untied their bonnets,
The bobolinks begun.
Then I said softly to myself,
"That must have been the sun!"

But how he set, I know not.
There seemed a purple stile
Which little yellow boys and girls
Were climbing all the while

Till when they reached the other side,
A dominie in gray
Put gently up the evening bars,
And led the flock away.

THE TIGER
WILLIAM BLAKE

Tiger! Tiger! burning bright
In the forests of the night,
What immortal hand or eye
Could frame thy fearful symmetry?

In what distant deeps or skies
Burnt the fire of thine eyes?
On what wings dare he aspire?
What the hand dare seize the fire?

And what shoulder, and what art,
Could twist the sinews of thy heart?
And when thy heart began to beat,
What dread hand forged thy dread feet?

What the hammer? what the chain?
In what furnace was thy brain?
What the anvil? what dread grasp?
Dare its deadly terrors clasp?

When the stars threw down their spears,
And watered heaven with their tears,
Did he smile his work to see?
Did he who made the Lamb make thee?

Tiger! Tiger! burning bright
In the forests of the night,
What immortal hand or eye,
Dare frame thy fearful symmetry?

FROM THE PRAIRIES
WILLIAM CULLEN BRYANT

These are the gardens of the Desert, these
The unshorn fields, boundless and beautiful,
For which the speech of England has no name—
The Prairies. I behold them for the first,
And my heart swells, while the dilated sight
Takes in the encircling vastness. Lo! they stretch,
In airy undulations, far away,

As if the ocean, in his gentlest swell,
Stood still, with all his rounded billows fixed,
And motionless forever.—Motionless?—
No—they are all unchained again. The clouds
Sweep over with their shadows, and, beneath,
The surface rolls and fluctuates to the eye;
Dark hollows seem to glide along and chase
The sunny ridges. Breezes of the South!

FROM SONG OF MYSELF
WALT WHITMAN

A child said *What is the grass?*
   fetching it to me with full hands.
How could I answer the child?
   I do not know what it is any more than he.

I guess it must be the flag of my disposition,
   out of hopeful green stuff woven.

Or I guess it is the handkerchief of the Lord,
A scented gift and remembrancer designedly dropt,
Bearing the owner's name someway in the corners,
   that we may see and remark, and say *Whose?*

Or I guess the grass is itself a child,
   the produced babe of the vegetation.

MOWING
ROBERT FROST

There was never a sound beside the wood but one,
And that was my long scythe whispering to the ground.
What was it it whispered? I knew not well myself;
Perhaps it was something about the heat of the sun,
Something, perhaps, about the lack of sound—
And that was why it whispered and did not speak.
It was no dream of the gift of idle hours,
Or easy gold at the hand of fay or elf:
Anything more than the truth would have seemed too weak
To the earnest love that laid the swale in rows,
Not without feeble-pointed spikes of flowers
(Pale orchises), and scared a bright green snake.
The fact is the sweetest dream that labor knows.
My long scythe whispered and left the hay to make.

GOD'S GRANDEUR
GERARD MANLEY HOPKINS

The world is charged with the grandeur of God
It will flame out, like shining from shook foil;
It gathers to a greatness, like the ooze of oil
Crushed. Why do men then now not reck his rod?
Generations have trod, have trod, have trod;
And all is seared with trade; bleared, smeared with toil;
And wears man's smudge and shares man's smell: the soil
Is bare now, nor can foot feel, being shod.
And for all this, nature is never spent;
There lives the dearest freshness deep down things;
And though the last lights off the black West went
Oh, morning, at the brown brink eastward, springs—
Because the Holy Ghost over the bent
World broods with warm breast and with ah! bright wings.

STOPPING BY WOODS ON A SNOWY EVENING
ROBERT FROST

Whose woods these are I think I know.
His house is in the village, though;
He will not see me stopping here
To watch his woods fill up with snow.

My little horse must think it queer
To stop without a farmhouse near
Between the woods and frozen lake
The darkest evening of the year.

He gives his harness bells a shake
To ask if there is some mistake.
The only other sound's the sweep
Of easy wind and downy flake.

The woods are lovely, dark, and deep,
But I have promises to keep,
And miles to go before I sleep,
And miles to go before I sleep.

OCTOBER'S BRIGHT BLUE WEATHER
HELEN HUNT JACKSON

O suns and skies and clouds of June,
    And flowers of June together,
Ye cannot rival for one hour
    October's bright blue weather.

When loud the humblebee makes haste,
    Belated, thriftless vagrant,
And Golden Rod is dying fast,
    And lanes with grapes are fragrant;

When all the lovely wayside things
    Their white-winged seeds are sowing,
And in the fields, still green and fair,
    Late aftermaths are growing;

When springs run low, and on the brooks,
    In idle golden freighting,
Bright leaves sink noiseless in the hush
    Of woods, for winter waiting;

When comrades seek sweet country haunts,
    By twos and twos together,
And count like misers, hour by hour,
    October's bright blue weather.

O suns and skies and flowers of June,
    Count all your boasts together,
Love loveth best of all the year
    October's bright blue weather.

To Autumn
JOHN KEATS

Season of mists and mellow fruitfulness,
    Close bosom-friend of the maturing sun;
Conspiring with him how to load and bless
    With fruit the vines that round the thatch-eves run;
To bend with apples the mossed cottage-trees,
    And fill all fruit with ripeness to the core;
        To swell the gourd, and plump the hazel shells
With a sweet kernel; to set budding more,
    And still more, later flowers for the bees,
    Until they think warm days will never cease,
        For Summer has o'er-brimmed their clammy cells.

Where are the songs of Spring? Ay, where are they?
    Think not of them, thou hast thy music too,—
While barred clouds bloom the soft-dying day,
    And touch the stubble-plains with rosy hue;
Then in a wailful choir the small gnats mourn
    Among the river sallows, borne aloft
        Or sinking as the light wind lives or dies;
And full-grown lambs loud bleat from hilly bourn;
    Hedge-crickets sing; and now with treble soft
    The red-breast whistles from a garden-croft;
        And gathering swallows twitter in the skies.

Reluctance
ROBERT FROST

Out through the fields and the woods
    And over the walls I have wended;
I have climbed the hills of view
    And looked at the world, and descended;
I have come by the highway home,
    And lo, it is ended.

The leaves are all dead on the ground,
    Save those that the oak is keeping
To ravel them one by one
    And let them go scraping and creeping
Out over the crusted snow,
    When others are sleeping.

And the dead leaves lie huddled and still,
    No longer blown hither and thither;
The last lone aster is gone;
    The flowers of the witch hazel wither;
The heart is still aching to seek,
    But the feet question "Whither?"

Ah, when to the heart of man
    Was it ever less than a treason
To go with the drift of things,
    To yield with a grace to reason,
And bow and accept the end
    Of a love or a season?

Fog
CARL SANDBURG

The fog comes
on little cat feet.

It sits looking
over harbor and city
on silent haunches
and then moves on.

THE SNOW-STORM
RALPH WALDO EMERSON

Announced by all the trumpets of the sky,
Arrives the snow, and, driving o'er the fields,
Seems nowhere to alight: the whited air
Hides hills and woods, the river, and the heaven,
And veils the farm-house at the garden's end.
The sled and traveller stopped, the courier's feet
Delayed, all friends shut out, the housemates sit
Around the radiant fireplace, enclosed
In a tumultuous privacy of storm.

Come see the north wind's masonry.
Out of an unseen quarry evermore
Furnished with tile, the fierce artificer
Curves his white bastions with projected roof
Round every windward stake, or tree, or door.

Speeding, the myriad-handed, his wild work
So fanciful, so savage, nought cares he
For number or proportion. Mockingly,
On coop or kennel he hangs Parian wreaths;
A swan-like form invests the hidden thorn;
Fills up the farmer's lane from wall to wall,
Maugre the farmer's sighs; and at the gate
A tapering turret overtops the work.
And when his hours are numbered, and the world
Is all his own, retiring, as he were not,
Leaves, when the sun appears, astonished Art
To mimic in slow structures, stone by stone,
Built in an age, the mad wind's night-work,
The frolic architecture of the snow.

THE FIRST SNOW-FALL
JAMES RUSSELL LOWELL

The snow had begun in the gloaming,
    And busily all the night
Had been heaping field and highway
    With a silence deep and white.

Every pine and fir and hemlock
    Wore ermine too dear for an earl,
And the poorest twig on the elm-tree
    Was ridged inch deep with pearl.

I stood and watched by the window
    The noiseless work of the sky,
And the sudden flurries of snow-birds,
    Like brown leaves whirling by.

I thought of a mound in sweet Auburn
    Where a little headstone stood;
How the flakes were folding it gently,
    As did robins the babes in the wood.

Up spoke our own little Mabel,
    Saying, "Father, who makes it snow?"
And I told of the good All-father
    Who cares for us here below.

Again I looked at the snow-fall,
    And thought of the leaden sky
That arched o'er our first great sorrow,
    When that mound was heaped so high.

I remembered the gradual patience
    That fell from that cloud like snow,
Flake by flake, healing and hiding
    The scar that renewed our woe.

And again to the child I whispered,
    "The snow that husheth all,
Darling, the merciful Father
    Alone can make it fall!"

Then, with eyes that saw not, I kissed her;
    And she, kissing back, could not know
That *my* kiss was given to her sister,
    Folded close under deepening snow.

SNOW-FLAKES
HENRY WADSWORTH LONGFELLOW

Out of the bosom of the Air,
   Out of the cloud-folds of her garments shaken,
Over the woodlands brown and bare,
   Over the harvest-fields forsaken,
     Silent, and soft, and slow
     Descends the snow.

This is the poem of the air,
   Slowly in silent syllables recorded;
This is the secret of despair,
   Long in its cloudy bosom hoarded,
     Now whispered and revealed
     To wood and field.

THE TIDE RISES, THE TIDE FALLS
HENRY WADSWORTH LONGFELLOW

The tide rises, the tide falls,
The twilight darkens, the curlew calls;
Along the sea-sands damp and brown
The traveller hastens toward the town,
   And the tide rises, the tide falls.

Darkness settles on roofs and walls,
But the sea, the sea in the darkness calls;
The little waves, with their soft, white hands,
Efface the footprints in the sands,
   And the tide rises, the tide falls.

The morning breaks; the steeds in their stalls
Stamp and neigh, as the hostler calls;
The day returns, but nevermore
Returns the traveller to the shore,
   And the tide rises, the tide falls.

The north wind's masonry

Words of

CROSSING THE BAR
ALFRED, LORD TENNYSON

Sunset and evening star,
And one clear call for me!

And may there be no moaning of the bar,
When I put out to sea,
But such a tide as moving seems asleep,
Too full for sound and foam,
When that which drew from out the boundless deep

Courage

Turns again home.
Twilight and evening bell,
And after that the dark!
And may there be no sadness of farewell,
When I embark;

For tho' from out our bourne of Time and Place
The flood may bear me far,
I hope to see my Pilot face to face
When I have crossed the bar.

SEVEN AGES OF MAN
FROM AS YOU LIKE IT
WILLIAM SHAKESPEARE

    All the world's a stage,
And all the men and women merely players.
They have their exits and their entrances,
And one man in his time plays many parts,
His acts being seven ages. At first, the infant,
Mewling and puking in the nurse's arms.
Then the whining schoolboy, with his satchel
And shining morning face, creeping like snail
Unwillingly to school. And then the lover,
Sighing like furnace, with a woeful ballad
Made to his mistress' eyebrow. Then a soldier,
Full of strange oaths and bearded like the pard,
Jealous in honor, sudden and quick in quarrel,
Seeking the bubble reputation
Even in the cannon's mouth. And then the justice,
In fair round belly with good capon lined,
With eyes severe and beard of formal cut,
Full of wise saws and modern instances;
And so he plays his part. The sixth age shifts
Into the lean and slippered pantaloon,
With spectacles on nose and pouch on side;
His youthful hose, well saved, a world too wide
For his shrunk shank, and his big manly voice,
Turning again toward childish trebel, pipes
And whistles in his sound. Last scene of all,
That ends this strange eventful history,
Is second childishness and mere oblivion,
Sans teeth, sans eyes, sans taste, sans everything.

This is my own . . .

THE MAN WHO THINKS HE CAN
WALTER D. WINTLE

If you think you are beaten, you are;
   If you think you dare not, you don't.
If you'd like to win, but think you can't,
   It's almost a cinch you won't.
If you think you'll lose, you're lost,
   For out in the world we find
Success begins with a fellow's will;
   It's all in the state of mind.

If you think you're outclassed, you are;
   You've got to think high to rise.
You've got to be sure of yourself before
   You can ever win a prize.
Life's battles don't always go
   To the stronger or faster man;
But soon or late the man who wins
   Is the one who thinks he can.

BREATHES THERE THE MAN WITH SOUL SO DEAD
FROM THE LAY OF THE LAST MINSTREL
SIR WALTER SCOTT

Breathes there the man with soul so dead
Who never to himself hath said,
This is my own, my native land!
Whose heart hath ne'er within him burned,
As home his footsteps he hath turned
From wandering on a foreign strand?
If such there breathe, go, mark him well;
For him no minstrel raptures swell;
High though his titles, proud his name,
Boundless his wealth as wish can claim,
Despite those titles, power, and pelf,
The wretch, concentred all in self,
Living, shall forfeit fair renown,
And, doubly dying, shall go down
To the vile dust from whence he sprung,
Unwept, unhonored, and unsung.

. . . my native land

One, if by land,

PAUL REVERE'S RIDE
HENRY WADSWORTH LONGFELLOW

Listen, my children, and you shall hear
Of the midnight ride of Paul Revere,
On the eighteenth of April, in Seventy-five;
Hardly a man is now alive
Who remembers that famous day and year.

He said to his friend, "If the British march
By land or sea from the town tonight,
Hang a lantern aloft in the belfry arch
Of the North Church tower as a signal light,—
One, if by land, and two, if by sea;
And I on the opposite shore will be,
Ready to ride and spread the alarm
Through every Middlesex village and farm,
For the country folk to be up and to arm."

Then he said, "Good night!" and with muffled oar
Silently rowed to the Charlestown shore,
Just as the moon rose over the bay,
Where swinging wide at her moorings lay
The *Somerset*, British man-of-war;
A phantom ship, with each mast and spar
Across the moon like a prison bar,
And a huge black hulk, that was magnified
By its own reflection in the tide.

Meanwhile, his friend through alley and street
Wanders and watches, with eager ears,
Till in the silence around him he hears
The muster of men at the barrack door,
The sound of arms, and the tramp of feet,
And the measured tread of the grenadiers,
Marching down to their boats on the shore.

Then he climbed the tower of the Old North Church,
By the wooden stairs, with stealthy tread,
To the belfry-chamber overhead,
And startled the pigeons from their perch
On the sombre rafters, that round him made
Masses and moving shapes of shade,—
By the trembling ladder, steep and tall,
To the highest window in the wall,
Where he paused to listen and look down
A moment on the roofs of the town
And the moonlight flowing over all.

Meanwhile, impatient to mount and ride,
Booted and spurred, with a heavy stride
On the opposite shore walked Paul Revere.
Now he patted his horse's side,
Now gazed at the landscape far and near,
Then, impetuous, stamped the earth,
And turned and tightened his saddle girth;
But mostly he watched with eager search
The belfry's tower of the Old North Church,
As it rose above the graves on the hill,
Lonely and spectral and sombre and still.
And lo! as he looks, on the belfry height
A glimmer, and then a gleam of light!
He springs to the saddle, the bridle he turns,
But lingers and gazes, till full on his sight
A second lamp in the belfry burns!

and two, if by sea . . .

A hurry of hoofs in a village street,
A shape in the moonlight, a bulk in the dark,
And beneath, from the pebbles, in passing, a spark
Struck out by a steed flying fearless and fleet;
That was all! And yet, through the gloom and the light,
The fate of a nation was riding that night;
And the spark struck out by that steed, in his flight,
Kindled the land into flame with its heat.
He has left the village and mounted the steep,
And beneath him, tranquil and broad and deep,
Is the Mystic, meeting the ocean tides;
And under the alders that skirt its edge,
Now soft on the sand, now loud on the ledge,
Is heard the tramp of his steed as he rides.

It was twelve by the village clock,
When he crossed the bridge into Medford town.
He heard the crowing of the cock,
And the barking of the farmer's dog,
And he felt the damp of the river fog,
That rises after the sun goes down.

It was one by the village clock,
When he galloped into Lexington.
He saw the gilded weathercock
Swim in the moonlight as he passed,
And the meeting-house windows, blank and bare,
Gaze at him with a spectral glare,
As if they already stood aghast
At the bloody work they would look upon.

It was two by the village clock,
When he came to the bridge in Concord town.
He heard the bleating of the flock,
And the twitter of birds among the trees,
And felt the breath of the morning breeze
Blowing over the meadows brown.
And one was safe and asleep in his bed
Who at the bridge would be first to fall,
Who that day would be lying dead,
Pierced by a British musket-ball.

You know the rest. In books you have read,
How the British Regulars fired and fled,—
How the farmers gave them ball for ball,
From behind each fence and farmyard wall,
Chasing the redcoats down the lane,
Then crossing the fields to emerge again
Under the trees at the turn of the road,
And only pausing to fire and load.

So through the night rode Paul Revere;
And so through the night went his cry of alarm
To every Middlesex village and farm,—
A cry of defiance, and not of fear,
A voice in the darkness, a knock at the door,
And a word that shall echo for evermore!
For, borne on the night-wind of the Past,
Through all our history, to the last,
In the hour of darkness and peril and need,
The people will waken and listen to hear
The hurrying hoof-beats of that steed,
And the midnight message of Paul Revere.

Barbara Frietchie
John Greenleaf Whittier

Up from the meadows rich with corn,
Clear in the cool September morn,

The clustered spires of Frederick stand
Green-walled by the hills of Maryland.

Fair as the garden of the Lord
To the eyes of the famished rebel horde,

On that pleasant morn of the early fall
When Lee marched over the mountain-wall;

Over the mountains winding down,
Horse and foot, into Frederick town.

Forty flags with their silver stars,
Forty flags with their crimson bars,

Flapped in the morning wind: the sun
Of noon looked down, and saw not one.

Up rose old Barbara Frietchie then,
Bowed with her fourscore years and ten;

Bravest of all in Frederick town,
She took up the flag the men hauled down;

In her attic window the staff she set,
To show that one heart was loyal yet.

Up the street came the rebel tread,
Stonewall Jackson riding ahead.

Under his slouched hat left and right
He glanced; the old flag met his sight.

"Halt!—the dust-brown ranks stood fast.
"Fire!"—out blazed the rifle-blast.

It shivered the window, pane and sash;
It rent the banner with seam and gash.

Quick as it fell, from the broken staff
Dame Barbara snatched the silken scarf.

She leaned far out on the window-sill,
And shook it forth with a royal will.

"Shoot, if you must, this old gray head,
But spare your country's flag," she said.

A shade of sadness, a blush of shame,
Over the face of the leader came;

The nobler nature within him stirred
To life at that woman's deed and word;

"Who touches a hair of yon gray head
Dies like a dog! March on!" he said.

All day long through Frederick street
Sounded the tread of marching feet:

All day long the free flag tost
Over the heads of the rebel host.

Ever its torn folds rose and fell
On the loyal winds that loved it well;

And through the hill-gaps sunset light
Shone over it with a warm good-night.

Barbara Frietchie's work is o'er,
And the Rebel rides on his raids no more.

Honor to her! and let a tear
Fall, for her sake, on Stonewall's bier.

Over Barbara Frietchie's grave,
Flag of Freedom and Union, wave!

Peace and order and beauty draw
Round thy symbol of light and law;

And ever the stars above look down
On thy stars below in Frederick town!

WANTED
JOSIAH GILBERT HOLLAND

God give us men! A time like this demands
   Strong minds, great hearts, true faith, and ready hands;
Men whom the lust of office does not kill;
   Men whom the spoils of office cannot buy;
Men who possess opinions and a will;
   Men who have honor,—men who will not lie;
Men who can stand before a demagogue,

And damn his treacherous flatteries without winking!
Tall men, sun-crowned, who live above the fog
   In public duty, and in private thinking;
For while the rabble, with their thumb-worn creeds,
Their large professions and their little deeds,—
Mingle in selfish strife, lo! Freedom weeps,
Wrong rules the land, and waiting Justice sleeps!

SAY NOT THE STRUGGLE NOUGHT AVAILETH
ARTHUR HUGH CLOUGH

Say not the struggle nought availeth,
   The labour and the wounds are vain,
The enemy faints not, nor faileth,
   And as things have been they remain.

If hopes were dupes, fears may be liars;
   It may be, in yon smoke concealed,
Your comrades chase e'en now the fliers,
   And, but for you, possess the field.

For while the tired waves, vainly breaking,
   Seem here no painful inch to gain,
Far back, through creeks and inlets making,
   Comes silent, flooding in, the main.

And not by eastern windows only,
   When daylight comes, comes in the light;
In front, the sun climbs slow, how slowly,
   But westward, look, the land is bright.

IN FLANDERS FIELDS
JOHN McCRAE

In Flanders fields the poppies blow
Between the crosses, row on row,
   That mark our place; and in the sky
   The larks, still bravely singing, fly
Scarce heard amid the guns below.

We are the Dead. Short days ago
We lived, felt dawn, saw sunset glow,
   Loved and were loved, and now we lie
   In Flanders fields.

Take up our quarrel with the foe:
To you from failing hands we throw
   The torch; be yours to hold it high.
   If ye break faith with us who die
We shall not sleep, though poppies grow
   In Flanders fields.

Fair is the garden of the Lord

One Step at a Time
Joseph Morris

In the morning with the journey all before us on the road,
  It takes courage to begin it, that is sure;
For the first step is the hardest, and we always think the load
  May be greater than we've power to endure.
When the first mile lies behind us we can say, "Now that is done,
  And the second and the third will soon be past."
So we trudge on through the noontime, and the setting of the sun
  Finds us coming to our stopping-place at last.

When a man would climb a mountain he's appalled to see the length
  Of the slope that reaches up into the sky;
But he starts, and with the climbing he will find he's gained the strength
  To attain the very top, however high.
For the climbing of a mountain takes but one step at a time—
  Who has courage to do that will reach the goal;
He will stand upon Life's summit and will know that joy sublime
  Which is his alone who dares to prove his soul.

Up and Doing
Douglas Malloch

Sure there is lots of trouble,
  Sure there are heaps of care,
Burdens that bend us double,
  Worries that come to wear.
But we must keep pursuing
  Something, and see it through;
Still to be up and doing
  Is all that there is to do.

Though you would like to idle,
  Wait for the world to right,
Keep your hand on the bridle,
  Fight when you have to fight.

Women are won by wooing,
  Fortune is won the same,
And to be up and doing
  Is all there is to the game.

Few ever fail by trying,
  Few ever win who wait.
All of your sitting, sighing
  Never will conquer fate.
Whatever path you're hewing,
  One thing is certain, son:
Either be up and doing
  Or soon you'll be down and done.

Do You Fear the Wind?
Hamlin Garland

Do you fear the force of the wind,
The slash of the rain?
Go face them and fight them,
Be savage again.
Go hungry and cold like the wolf,
    Go wade like the crane;
The palms of your hands will thicken,
The skin of your cheek will tan,
You'll grow ragged and weary and swarthy,
    But you'll walk like a man!

Begin Again
Susan Coolidge

Every day is a fresh beginning,
    Every day is the world made new;
You who are weary of sorrow and sinning,
    Here is a beautiful hope for you—
    A hope for me and a hope for you.

All the past things are past and over,
    The tasks are done and the tears are shed;
Yesterday's errors let yesterday cover;
    Yesterday's wounds, which smarted and bled,
    Are healed with the healing which night has shed.

Yesterday now is a part of forever,
    Bound up in a sheaf, which God holds tight;
With glad days, and sad days, and bad days which never
    Shall visit us more with their bloom and their blight,
    Their fullness of sunshine or sorrowful night.

Let them go, since we cannot relieve them,
    Cannot undo and cannot atone;
God in His mercy, receive, forgive them;
    Only the new days are our own,
    Today is ours, and today alone.

Every day is a fresh beginning;
    Listen, my soul, to the glad refrain,
And, spite of old sorrow and older sinning,
    And puzzles forecasted and possible pain
    Take heart with the day, and begin again.

Let's be brave when...

THE BRAVEST BATTLE
JOAQUIN MILLER

The bravest battle that ever was fought;
  Shall I tell you where and when?
On the maps of the world you will find it not;
  It was fought by the mothers of men.

Nay, not with cannon or battle shot,
  With sword or braver pen;
Nay, not with eloquent word or thought,
  From mouths of wonderful men,

But deep in a woman's walled-up heart—
  Of woman that would not yield,

But patiently, silently bore her part—
  Lo! there in that battlefield.

No marshaling troop, no bivouac song;
  No banner to gleam and wave;
And oh! these battles they last so long—
  From babyhood to the grave!

Yet, faithful still as a bridge of stars,
  She fights in her walled-up town—
Fights on and on in the endless wars,
  Then silent, unseen—goes down.

the laughter dies.

LET'S BE BRAVE
EDGAR A. GUEST

Let's be brave when the laughter dies
And the tears come into our troubled eyes,
Let's cling to the faith and the old belief
When the skies grow gray with the clouds of grief,
Let's bear the sorrow and hurt and pain
And wait till the laughter comes again.

Let's be brave when the trials come
And our hearts are sad and our lips are dumb,
Let's strengthen ourselves in the times of test
By whispering softly that God knows best;
Let us still believe, though we cannot know,
We shall learn sometime it is better so.

Let's be brave when the joy departs,
Till peace shall come to our troubled hearts,
For the tears must fall and the rain come down
And each brow be pressed to the thorny crown;
Yet after the dark shall the sun arise,
So let's be brave when the laughter dies.

TRUE HEROISM
AUTHOR UNKNOWN

Let others write of battles fought,
    Of bloody, ghastly fields,
Where honor greets the man who wins,
    And death the man who yields;
But I will write of him who fights
    And vanquishes his sins,
Who struggles on through weary years
    Against himself, and wins.

He is a hero staunch and brave
    Who fights an unseen foe,
And puts at last beneath his feet
    His passions base and low;
Who stands erect in manhood's might,
    Undaunted, undismayed,
The bravest man who ere drew sword
    In foray or in raid.

It calls for something more than brawn
    Or muscle, to o'ercome
An enemy who marcheth not
    With banner, plume, and drum;
He may not wear a hero's crown,
    Or fill a hero's grave,
But truth will place his name among
    The bravest of the brave.

I WOULD BE TRUE
HOWARD ARNOLD WALTER

I would be true, for there are those who trust me;
    I would be pure, for there are those who care;
I would be strong, for there is much to suffer;
    I would be brave, for there is much to dare.
I would be friend of all—the foe, the friendless;
    I would be giving and forget the gift.
I would be humble, for I know my weakness;
    I would look up—and laugh—and love—and lift.

The Speech Before Harfleur
from Henry V
William Shakespeare

Once more unto the breach, dear friends, once more;
Or close the wall up with our English dead!
In peace there's nothing so becomes a man,
As modest stillness and humility:
But when the blast of war blows in our ears,
Then imitate the action of the tiger;
Stiffen the sinews, summon up the blood,
Disguise fair nature with hard-favoured rage,
Then lend the eye a terrible aspect;
Let it pry through the portage of the head,
Like the brass cannon: let the brow o'erwhelm it,
As fearfully as doth a galled rock
O'erhang and jutty his confounded base
Swilled with the wild and wasteful ocean.
Now set the teeth, and stretch the nostril wide;
Hold hard the breath, and bend up every spirit
To his full height!—On, on, you noblest English!
Whose blood is fet from fathers of warproof;
Fathers that, like so many Alexanders,
Have in these parts from morn till even fought,
And sheathed their swords for lack of argument.
Dishonour not your mothers: now attest
That those whom you called fathers did beget you!
Be copy now to men of grosser blood,
And teach them how to war!—And you, good yeomen,
Whose limbs were made in England, show us here
The mettle of your pasture; let us swear
That you are worth your breeding, which I doubt not;
For there is none of you so mean and base
That hath not noble lustre in your eyes.
I see you stand like greyhounds in the slips,
Straining upon the start. The game's afoot;
Follow your spirit: and, upon this charge,
Cry—God for Harry! England and Saint George!

Follow your spirit . . .

COURAGE
39

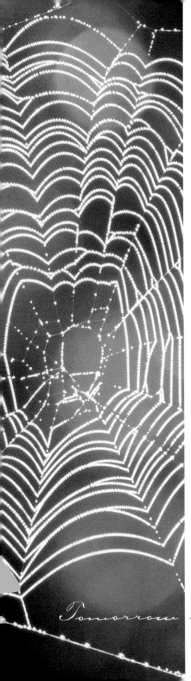

TRY, TRY AGAIN
AUTHOR UNKNOWN

'Tis a lesson you should heed,
   Try, try again;
If at first you don't succeed,
   Try, try again;
Then your courage should appear,
For, if you will persevere,
You will conquer, never fear;
   Try, try again.

Once or twice though you should fail,
   Try, try again;
If you would at last prevail,
   Try, try again;

If we strive, 'tis no disgrace
Though we do not win the race;
What should you do in the case?
   Try, try again.

Time will bring you your reward,
   Try, try again.
All that other folks can do,
Why, with patience, should not you?
Only keep this rule in view;
   Try, try again.

A NOISELESS PATIENT SPIDER
WALT WHITMAN

A noiseless patient spider,
I mark'd where on a little promontory
   it stood isolated,
Mark'd how to explore the vacant vast surrounding,
It launch'd forth filament, filament, filament,
   out of itself,
Ever unreeling them, ever tirelessly speeding them.

And you O my soul where you stand,
Surrounded, detached, in measureless
   oceans of space,
Ceaselessly musing, venturing, throwing,
   seeking the spheres to connect them,
Till the bridge you will need be form'd,
   till the ductile anchor hold,
Till the gossamer thread you fling
   catch somewhere, O my soul.

Tomorrow comes the song

CREDO
Edwin Arlington Robinson

I cannot find my way: there is no star
In all the shrouded heavens anywhere;
And there is not a whisper in the air
Of any living voice but one so far
That I can hear it only as a bar
Of lost, imperial music, played when fair
And angel fingers wove, and unaware,

Dead leaves to garlands where no roses are.
No, there is not a glimmer, nor a call,
For one that welcomes, welcomes when he fears,
The black and awful chaos of the night;
For through it all—above, beyond it all—
I know the far-sent message of the years,
I feel the coming glory of the Light.

THE SIN OF OMISSION
Margaret E. Sangster

It isn't the thing you do, dear,
    It's the thing you leave undone
That gives you a bit of a heartache
    At setting of the sun.
The tender word forgotten,
    The letter you did not write,
The flowers you did not send, dear,
    Are your haunting ghosts at night.

The stone you might have lifted
    Out of a brother's way;
The bit of heartsome counsel
    You were hurried too much to say;
The loving touch of the hand, dear,
    The gentle, winning tone
Which you had no time nor thought for
    With troubles enough of your own.

Those little acts of kindness
    So easily out of mind,
Those chances to be angels
    Which we poor mortals find—
They come in night and silence,
    Each sad, reproachful wraith,
When hope is faint and flagging,
    And a chill has fallen on faith.

For life is all too short, dear,
    And sorrow is all too great,
To suffer our slow compassion
    That tarries until too late;
And it isn't the thing you do, dear,
    It's the thing you leave undone
Which gives you a bit of a heartache
    At the setting of the sun.

BE STRONG
Maltbie Davenport Babcock

Be strong!
We are not here to play,—to dream, to drift.
We have hard work to do and loads to lift.
Shun not the struggle,—face it: 'tis God's gift.
    Be strong!

Say not the days are evil. Who's to blame?
And fold the hands and acquiesce,—O shame!
Stand up, speak out, and bravely, in God's name.
    Be strong!
It matters not how deep intrenched the wrong,
How hard the battle goes, the day how long;
Faint not,—fight on! To-morrow comes the song.

The tide is full,

An Inspiration
Ella Wheeler Wilcox

However the battle is ended,
   Though proudly the victor comes
With fluttering flags and prancing nags
   And echoing roll of drums,
Still truth proclaims this motto
   In letters of living light,—
No question is ever settled
   Until it is settled right.

Though the heel of the strong oppressor
   May grind the weak in the dust,
And the voices of fame with one acclaim
   May call him great and just,
Let those who applaud take warning,
   And keep this motto in sight,—
No question is ever settled
   Until it is settled right.

Let those who have failed take courage;
   Tho' the enemy seems to have won,
Tho' his ranks are strong, if he be in the wrong
   The battle is not yet done;
For, sure as the morning follows
   The darkest hour of the night,
No question is ever settled
   Until it is settled right.

O man bowed down with labor!
   O woman young, yet old!
O heart oppressed in the toiler's breast
   And crushed by the power of gold!
Keep on with your weary battle
   Against triumphant might;
No question is ever settled
   Until it is settled right.

the moon lies fair.

DOVER BEACH
MATTHEW ARNOLD

The sea is calm to-night.
The tide is full, the moon lies fair
Upon the straits; on the French coast the light
Gleams and is gone; the cliffs of England stand,
Glimmering and vast, out in the tranquil bay.
Come to the window, sweet is the night-air!
Only, from the long line of spray
Where the sea meets the moon-blanched land,
Listen! you hear the grating roar
Of pebbles which the waves draw back, and fling,
At their return, up the high strand,
Begin, and cease, and then again begin,
With tremulous cadence slow, and bring
The eternal note of sadness in.

Sophocles long ago
Heard it on the Ægæan, and it brought
Into his mind the turbid ebb and flow
Of human misery; we

Find also in the sound a thought,
Hearing it by this distant northern sea. The Sea of Faith
Was once, too, at the full, and round earth's shore
Lay like the folds of a bright girdle furled.
But now I only hear
Its melancholy, long, withdrawing roar,
Retreating, to the breath
Of the night-wind, down the vast edges drear
And naked shingles of the world.

Ah, Love, let us be true
To one another! for the world, which seems
To lie before us like a land of dreams,
So various, so beautiful, so new,
Hath really neither joy, nor love, nor light,
Nor certitude, nor peace, nor help for pain;
And we are here as on a darkling plain
Swept with confused alarms of struggle and flight,
Where ignorant armies clash by night.

The Leak in the Dike
Phoebe Cary

The good dame looked from her cottage
　　At the close of the pleasant day,
And cheerily called to her little son
　　Outside the door at play:
"Come, Peter! come! I want you to go,
　　While there is light to see,
To the hut of the blind old man who lives
　　Across the dike, for me;
And take these cakes I made for him—
　　They are hot and smoking yet;
You have time enough to go and come
　　Before the sun is set."

And Peter left the brother,
　　With whom all day he had played,
And the sister who had watched their sports
　　In the willow's tender shade;
And told them they'd see him back before
　　They saw a star in sight,
Though he wouldn't be afraid to go
　　In the very darkest night!
For he was a brave, bright fellow,
　　With eye and conscience clear;
He could do whatever a boy might do,
　　And he had not learned to fear.
Why, he wouldn't have robbed a bird's nest,
　　Nor brought a stork to harm,
Though never a law in Holland
　　Had stood to stay his arm!

And now with his face all glowing,
　　And eyes as bright as the day
With the thoughts of his pleasant errand,
　　He trudged along the way;
And soon his joyous prattle
　　Made glad a lonesome place—

Alas! if only the blind old man
　　Could have seen that happy face!
Yet he somehow caught the brightness
　　Which his voice and presence lent
And he felt the sunshine come and go
　　As Peter came and went.

And now, as the day was sinking,
　　And the winds began to rise,
The mother looked from her door again,
　　Shading her anxious eyes,
And saw the shadows deepen
　　And birds to their home come back,
But never a sign of Peter
　　Along the level track.
But she said: "He will come at morning,
　　So I need not fret or grieve—
Though it isn't like my boy at all
　　To stay without my leave."

But where was the child delaying?
　　On the homeward way was he,
And across the dike while the sun was up
　　An hour above the sea.
He was stopping now to gather flowers,
　　Now listening to the sound,
As the angry waters dashed themselves
　　Against their narrow bound.
But hark! through the noise of waters
　　Comes a low, clear, trickling sound;
And the child's face pales with terror,
　　And his blossoms drop to the ground.
He is up the bank in a moment,
　　And, stealing through the sand,
He sees a stream not yet so large
　　As his slender, childish hand.

Give thanks for your son . . .

'Tis a leak in the dike!—He is but a boy,
  Unused to fearful scenes;
But, young as he is, he has learned to know
  The dreadful thing that means.
A leak in the dike! The stoutest heart
  Grows faint that cry to hear,
And the bravest man in all the land
  Turns white with mortal fear.
For he knows the smallest leak may grow
  To a flood in a single night;
And he knows the strength of the cruel sea
  When loosed in its angry might.

And the Boy! he has seen the danger
  And, shouting a wild alarm,
He forces back the weight of the sea
  With the strength of his single arm!
He listens for the joyful sound
  Of a footstep passing nigh;
And lays his ear to the ground, to catch
  The answer to his cry.
And he hears the rough winds blowing,
  And the waters rise and fall,
But never an answer comes to him
  Save the echo of his call.
He sees no hope, no succor,
  His feeble voice is lost;
Yet what shall he do but watch and wait
  Though he perish at his post!

So, faintly calling and crying
  Till the sun is under the sea;
Crying and moaning till the stars
  Come out for company;
He thinks of his brother and sister,
  Asleep in their safe warm bed;
He thinks of his father and mother,
  Of himself as dying—and dead;

And of how, when the night is over,
  They must come and find him at last;
But he never thinks he can leave the place
  Where duty holds him fast.
The good dame in the cottage
  Is up and astir with the light,
For the thought of her little Peter
  Has been with her all night.
And now she watches the pathway,
  As yester-eve she had done;
But what does she see so strange and black
  Against the rising sun?
Her neighbors are bearing between them
  Something straight to her door;
Her child is coming home, but not
  As he ever came before!

"He is dead!" she cries, "my darling!"
  And the startled father hears,
And comes and looks the way she looks,
  And fears the thing she fears;
Till a glad shout from the bearers
  Thrills the stricken man and wife—
"Give thanks, for your son has saved our land,
  And God has saved his life!"
So, there in the morning sunshine
  They knelt about the boy;
And every head was bared and bent
  In tearful, reverent joy.

'Tis many a year since then; but still,
  When the sea roars like a flood,
The boys are taught what a boy can do
  Who is brave and true and good;
For every man in that country
  Takes his son by the hand
And tells him of little Peter,
  Whose courage saved the land.

. . . has saved our land!

Fear No More the Heat o' the Sun
from Cymbeline
William Shakespeare

Fear no more the heat o' the sun,
   Nor the furious winter's rages;
Thou thy worldly task hast done,
   Home art gone, and ta'en thy wages;
Golden lads and girls all must,
As chimney-sweepers, come to dust.

Fear no more the frown o' the great,
   Thou art past the tyrant's stroke;
Care no more to clothe and eat,
   To thee the reed is as the oak.
The scepter, learning, physic, must
All follow this and come to dust.

Reliance
Henry van Dyke

Not to the swift, the race:
   Not to the strong, the fight:
Not to the righteous, perfect grace:
   Not to the wise, the light.

But often faltering feet
   Come surest to the goal;
And they who walk in darkness meet
   The sunrise of the soul.

The truth the wise men sought
   Was spoken by a child;
The alabaster box was brought
   In trembling hands defiled.

Not from my torch, the gleam,
   But from the stars above:
Not from my heart, life's crystal stream,
   But from the depths of Love.

Do Not Go Gentle into That Good Night
Dylan Thomas

Do not go gentle into that good night,
Old age should burn and rave at close of day;
Rage, rage against the dying of the light.

Though wise men at their end know dark is right,
Because their words had forked no lightning they
Do not go gentle into that good night.

Good men, the last wave by, crying how bright
Their frail deeds might have danced in a green bay,
Rage, rage against the dying of the light.

Wild men who caught and sang the sun in flight,
And learn, too late, they grieved it on its way,
Do not go gentle into that good night.

Grave men, near death, who see with blinding sight
Blind eyes could blaze like meteors and be gay,
Rage, rage against the dying of the light.

And you, my father, there on the sad height,
Curse, bless, me now with your fierce tears, I pray.
Do not go gentle into that good night.
Rage, rage against the dying of the light.

Sea Fever
John Masefield

I must go down to the seas again, to the lonely sea and the sky,
And all I ask is a tall ship and a star to steer her by,
And the wheel's kick and the wind's song and the white sail's shaking,
And a gray mist on the sea's face, and a gray dawn breaking.

I must go down to the seas again, for the call of the running tide
Is a wild call and a clear call that may not be denied;
And all I ask is a windy day with the white clouds flying,
And the flung spray and the blown spume, and the sea-gulls crying.

I must go down to the seas again, to the vagrant gypsy life,
To the gull's way and the whale's way, where the wind's like a whetted knife;
And all I ask is a merry yarn from a laughing fellow-rover,
And quiet sleep and a sweet dream when the long trick's over.

DEATH BE NOT PROUD
JOHN DONNE

Death be not proud, though some have called thee
Mighty and dreadfull, for thou art not soe,
For those whom thou think'st thou dost overthrow
Die not, poore death, nor yet canst thou kill mee.
From rest and sleepe, which but thy pictures bee,
Much pleasure, then from thee, much more must flow,
And soonest our best men with thee doe goe,
Rest of their bones, and soules deliverie.
Thou art slave to Fate, Chance, kings, and desperate men,
And dost with poyson, warre, and sicknesse dwell,
And poppie, or charmes can make us sleepe as well,
And better than thy stroake; why swell'st thou then?
One short sleepe past, wee wake eternally,
And death shall be no more; death, thou shalt die.

PROSPICE
ROBERT BROWNING

Fear death?—to feel the fog in my throat,
    The mist in my face,
When the snows begin, and the blasts denote
    I am nearing the place,
The power of the night, the press of the storm,
    The post of the foe;
Where he stands, the Arch Fear in a visible form,
    Yet the strong man must go . . .
For sudden the worst turns the best to the brave,
    The black minute's at end,
And the elements' rage, the fiend-voices that rave,
    Shall dwindle, shall blend,
Shall change, shall become first a peace out of pain,
    Then a light, then thy breast,
O thou soul of my soul! I shall clasp thee again,
    And with God be the rest!

Poems for

I Remember, I Remember
Thomas Hood

I remember, I remember,
　The house where I was born
The little window where the sun
　Came peeping in at morn:
He never came a wink too soon,
　Nor brought too long a day;

But now, I often wish the night
　Had borne my breath away.
I remember, I remember,
　The roses, red and white;
The violets, and the lily-cups,
　Those flowers made of light!
The lilacs where the robin built,
　And where my brother set
The laburnum on his birthday,—

Families

The tree is living yet!
I remember, I remember,
    Where I used to swing;
And thought the air must rush as fresh
    To swallows on the wing:
My spirit flew in feathers then,
    That is so heavy now,
And summer pools could hardly cool
    The fever on my brow!

I remember, I remember,
    The fir trees dark and high;
I used to think their slender tops
    Were close against the sky:
It was a childish ignorance,
    But now 'tis little joy
To know I'm farther off from heaven
    Than when I was a boy.

HOME
EDGAR A. GUEST

It takes a heap o' livin' in a house t' make it home,
A heap o' sun an' shadder, an' ye sometimes have t' roam
Afore ye really 'preciate the things ye lef' behind,
An' hunger fer 'em somehow, with 'em allus on yer mind.
It don't make any differunce how rich ye get t' be,
How much yer chairs an' tables cost, how great yer luxury;
It ain't home t' ye, though it be the palace of a king,
Until somehow yer soul is sort o' wrapped round everything.

Home ain't a place that gold can buy or get up in a minute;
Afore it's home there's got t' be a heap o' livin' in it;
Within the walls there's got t' be some babies born, and then
Right there ye've got t' bring 'em up t' women good, an' men;
And gradjerly, as time goes on, ye find ye wouldn't part
With anything they ever used—they've grown into yer heart:
The old high chairs, the playthings, too, the little shoes they wore
Ye hoard; an' if ye could ye'd keep the thumb-marks on the door.

Ye've got t' weep t' make it home, ye've got t' sit an' sigh
An' watch beside a loved one's bed, an' know that Death is nigh;
An' in the stillness o' the night t' see Death's angel come,
An' close the eyes o' her that smiled, an' leave her sweet voice dumb.
For these are scenes that grip the heart, an' when yer tears are dried,
Ye find the home is dearer than it was, an' sanctified;
An' tuggin' at ye always are the pleasant memories
O' her that was an' is no more—ye can't escape from these.

Ye've got to sing an' dance fer years, ye've got t' romp an' play,
An' learn t' love the things ye have by usin' 'em each day;
Even the roses round the porch must blossom year by year
Afore they 'come a part o' ye, suggestin' someone dear
Who used t' love 'em long ago, and trained 'em just t' run
The way they do, so's they would get the early mornin' sun;
Ye've got to love each brick an' stone from cellar up t' dome:
It takes a heap o' livin' in a house t' make it home.

JUST FOLKS
EDGAR A. GUEST

We're queer folks here.
We'll talk about the weather,
The good times we've had together,
The good times near,
The roses buddin', an' the bees
Once more upon their nectar sprees;
The scarlet fever scare, an' who
Came mighty near not pullin' through,
An' who had light attacks, an' all
The things that int'rest, big or small;
But here you'll never hear of sinnin'
Or any scandal that's beginnin'.
We've got too many other labors
To scatter tales that harm our neighbors.

We've one rule here,
An' that is to be pleasant.
The folks we know are always present,
Or very near.
An' though they dwell in many places,
We think we're talkin' to their faces;
An' that keeps us from only seein'
The faults in any human bein',
An' checks our tongues when they'd go trailin'
Into the mire of mortal failin'.
Flaws aren't so big when folks are near you;
You don't talk mean when they can hear you.
An' so no scandal here is started,
Because from friends we're never parted.

SITTIN' ON THE PORCH
EDGAR A. GUEST

Sittin' on the porch at night
   when all the tasks are done,
Just restin' there and talkin',
   with my easy slippers on,
An' my shirt band thrown wide open
   an' my feet upon the rail,
Oh, it's then I'm at my richest,
   with a wealth that cannot fail;
For the scent of early roses
   seems to flood the evening air,
An' a throne of downright gladness
   is my wicker rocking-chair.

The dog asleep beside me,
   an' the children rompin' round,
With their shrieks of merry laughter,
   oh, there is no gladder sound
To the ears o' weary mortals
   spite of all the scoffers say,
Or a grander bit of music
   than the children at their play!
An' I tell myself times over,
   when I'm sittin' there at night,
That the world in which I'm livin'
   is a place o' real delight.

Then the moon begins its climbin'
   an' the stars shine overhead,
An' the mother calls the children
   an' she takes 'em up to bed,
An' I smoke my pipe in silence
   an' I think o' many things,
An' balance up my riches
   with the lonesomeness o' kings,
An' I come to this conclusion,
   an' I'll wager that I'm right—
That I'm happier than they are
   sittin' on my porch at night.

Wealth that cannot fail

Where did you get

THE HAND THAT ROCKS THE CRADLE
IS THE HAND THAT RULES THE WORLD
WILLIAM ROSS WALLACE

Blessings on the hand of women!
Angels guard its strength and grace,
In the palace, cottage, hovel,
Oh, no matter where the place;
Would that never storms assailed it,
Rainbows ever gently curled;
For the hand that rocks the cradle
Is the hand that rules the world.
Infancy's the tender fountain,
Power may with beauty flow,
Mother's first to guide the streamlets,
From them souls unresting grow—
Grow on for the good or evil,
Sunshine streamed or evil hurled;
For the hand that rocks the cradle
Is the hand that rules the world.

Woman, how divine your mission
Here upon our natal sod!
Keep, oh, keep the young heart open
Always to the breath of God!
All true trophies of the ages
Are from mother-love impearled;
For the hand that rocks the cradle
Is the hand that rules the world.
Blessings on the hand of women!
Fathers, sons, and daughters cry,
And the sacred song is mingled
With the worship in the sky—
Mingles where no tempest darkens,
Rainbows evermore are hurled;
For the hand that rocks the cradle
Is the hand that rules the world.

your eyes so blue?

WHERE DID YOU COME FROM?
GEORGE MACDONALD

Where did you come from, Baby dear?
Out of the everywhere into here.

Where did you get your eyes so blue?
Out of the sky as I came through.

What makes the light in them sparkle and spin?
Some of the starry spikes left in.

Where did you get that little tear?
I found it waiting when I got here.

What makes your forehead so smooth and high?
A soft hand stroked it as I went by.

What makes your cheek like a warm white rose?
I saw something better than anyone knows.

Whence that three-corner'd smile of bliss?
Three angels gave me at once a kiss.

Where did you get this pearly ear?
God spoke, and it came out to hear.

Where did you get those arms and hands?
Love made itself into hooks and bands.

Feet, whence did you come, you darling things?
From the same box as the cherubs' wings.

How did they all come just to be you?
God thought of me, and so I grew.

But how did you come to us, you dear?
God thought of you, and so I am here.

Dreams for
a penny

LULLABY TOWN
John Irving Diller

There's a quaint little place they call Lullaby Town—
It's just back of those hills where the sunsets go down.
Its streets are of silver, its buildings of gold,
And its palaces dazzling things to behold;
There are dozens of spires, housing musical chimes;
Its people are folk from the Nursery Rimes,
And at night it's alight, like a garden of gleams,
With fairies, who bring the most wonderful dreams.

The Sandman is Mayor, and he rules like a King.
The climate's so balmy that, always, it's spring,
And it's never too cold, and it's never too hot,
And I'm told that there's nowhere a prettier spot;
All in and about it are giant old trees,
Filled with radiant birds that will sing when you please;
But the strange thing about it—this secret, pray, keep—
Is, it never awakes till the world is asleep.

So when night settles down, all its lights snap aglow,
And its streets fill with people who dance to and fro.
Mother Goose, Old King Cole and his fiddlers three,
Miss Muffet, Jack Sprat and his wife, scamper free,
With a whole host of others, a boisterous crew,
Not forgetting the Old Lady Who Lived in a Shoe
And her troublesome brood who, with brownie and sprite,
Go trooping the streets, a bewildering sight.

There's a peddler who carries, strapped high on his back,
A bundle. Now, guess what he has in that pack.
There's a crowd all about him a-buying his wares,
And they're grabbing his goods up in threes and in pairs.
No, he's not peddling jams nor delectable creams.
Would you know what he's selling? Just wonderful dreams!

There are dreams for a penny and dreams that cost two;
And there's no two alike, and they're sure to come true;
And the buyers fare off with a toss of the head,
And they visit the Sandman, then hie them to bed;
For there's nothing to do in this land of Bo-Peep,
But to frolic and sing and then go off to sleep!

The Lamplighter
Robert Louis Stevenson

My tea is nearly ready and the sun has left the sky;
It's time to take the window to see Leerie going by;
For every night at teatime and before you take your seat,
With lantern and with ladder he comes posting up the street.

Now Tom would be a driver and Maria go to sea,
And my papa's a banker and as rich as he can be;
But I, when I am stronger and can choose what I'm to do,
O Leerie, I'll go round at night and light the lamps with you!

For we are very lucky, with a lamp before the door,
And Leerie stops to light it as he lights so many more;
And O, before you hurry by with ladder and with light,
O Leerie, see a little child and nod to him to-night!

Dream Variation
Langston Hughes

To fling my arms wide
In some place of the sun,
To whirl and to dance
Till the white day is done.
Then rest at cool evening
Beneath a tall tree
While night comes on gently,
    Dark like me—
That is my dream!

To fling my arms wide
In the face of the sun,
Dance! whirl! whirl!
Till the quick day is done.
Rest at pale evening . . .
A tall, slim tree, . . .
Night coming tenderly,
    Black like me.

*and dreams
that cost two.*

THE LAND OF STORY-BOOKS
Robert Louis Stevenson

At evening when the lamp is lit,
Around the fire my parents sit;
They sit at home and talk and sing,
And do not play at anything.

Now, with my little gun, I crawl
All in the dark along the wall,
And follow round the forest track
Away behind the sofa back.

There, in the night, where none can spy,
All in my hunter's camp I lie,
And play at books that I have read
Till it is time to go to bed.

These are the hills, these are the woods,
These are my starry solitudes;
And there the river by whose brink
The roaring lions come to drink.

I see the others far away
As if in firelit camp they lay,
And I, like to an Indian scout,
Around their party prowled about.

So, when my nurse comes in for me,
Home I return across the sea,
And go to bed with backward looks
At my dear land of Story-books.

THE CHILDREN'S HOUR
Henry Wadsworth Longfellow

Between the dark and the daylight,
    When the night is beginning to lower,
Comes a pause in the day's occupations,
    That is known as the Children's Hour.

I hear in the chamber above me
    The patter of little feet,
The sound of a door that is opened,
    And voices soft and sweet.

From my study I see in the lamplight,
    Descending the broad hall stair,
Grave Alice, and laughing Allegra,
    And Edith with golden hair.

A whisper, and then a silence:
    Yet I know by their merry eyes
They are plotting and planning together
    To take me by surprise.

A sudden rush from the stairway,
    A sudden raid from the hall!
By three doors left unguarded
    They enter my castle wall!

They climb up into my turret
    O'er the arms and back of my chair
If I try to escape, they surround me
    They seem to be everywhere.

They almost devour me with kisses,
    Their arms about me entwine,
Till I think of the Bishop of Bingen,
    In his Mouse-Tower on the Rhine.

Do you think, O blue-eyed banditti,
    Because you have scaled the wall,
Such an old mustache as I am
    Is not a match for you all!

I have you fast in my fortress,
    And will not let you depart,
But put you down into the dungeon
    In the round-tower of my heart.

And there will I keep you forever,
    Yes, forever and a day,
Till the walls shall crumble to ruin,
    And moulder in dust away!

THE SUGAR-PLUM TREE
EUGENE FIELD

Have you ever heard of the Sugar-Plum Tree?
'Tis a marvel of great renown!
It blooms on the shore of the Lollypop Sea
In the garden of Shut-Eye Town;
The fruit that it bears is so wondrously sweet
(As those who have tasted it say)
That good little children have only to eat
Of that fruit to be happy next day.

When you've got to the tree, you would have a hard time
To capture the fruit which I sing;
The tree is so tall that no person could climb
To the boughs where the sugar-plums swing!
But up in that tree sits a chocolate cat,
And a gingerbread dog prowls below—
And this is the way you contrive to get at
Those sugar-plums tempting you so:

You say but the word to that gingerbread dog
And he barks with such a terrible zest
That the chocolate cat is at once all agog,
As her swelling proportions attest.
And the chocolate cat goes cavorting around
From this leafy limb unto that,
And the sugar-plums tumble, of course, to the ground—
Hurrah for that chocolate cat!

There are marshmallows, gumdrops, and peppermint canes
With stripings of scarlet and gold,
And you carry away of the treasure that rains,
As much as your apron can hold!
So come, little child, cuddle closer to me
In your dainty white nightcap and gown,
And I'll rock you away to that Sugar-Plum Tree
In the garden of Shut-Eye Town.

LITTLE BOY BLUE
EUGENE FIELD

The little toy dog is covered with dust,
    But sturdy and stanch he stands;
And the little toy soldier is red with rust,
    And his musket molds in his hands.
Time was when the little toy dog was new
    And the soldier was passing fair,
And that was the time when our Little Boy Blue
    Kissed them and put them there.

"Now, don't you go till I come," he said,
    "And don't you make any noise!"
So toddling off to his trundle-bed
    He dreamed of the pretty toys.
And as he was dreaming, an angel song
    Awakened our Little Boy Blue—
Oh, the years are many, the years are long,
    But the little toy friends are true.

Aye, faithful to Little Boy Blue they stand,
    Each in the same old place,
Awaiting the touch of a little hand,
    And the smile of a little face.
And they wonder, as waiting these long years through,
    In the dust of that little chair,
What has become of our Little Boy Blue
    Since he kissed them and put them there.

The early lilacs . . .

FROM THERE WAS A CHILD WENT FORTH
WALT WHITMAN

There was a child went forth every day,
And the first object he looked upon,
    that object he became,
And that object became part of him
    for the day or a certain part of the day,
Or for many years or stretching cycles of years.
The early lilacs became part of this child,
And grass and white and red morning-glories,
    and white and red clover, and the song of the phoebe-bird,
And the Third-month lambs and the sow's pink-faint litter,
    and the mare's foal and the cow's calf,
And the noisy brood of the barnyard
    or by the mire of the pond-side,
And the fish suspending themselves so curiously below there,
    and the beautiful curious liquid,
And the water-plants with their graceful flat heads,
    all became part of him.

  The field-sprouts of Fourth-month
    and Fifth-month became part of him,
Winter-grain sprouts and those of the light-yellow corn,
    and the esculent roots of the garden,
And the apple-trees covered with blossoms and the fruit afterward,
    and woodberries, and the commonest weeds by the road, . . .
And all the changes of city and country wherever he went.

His own parents, he that had fathered him
    and she that had conceived him in her womb and birthed him,
They gave this child more of themselves than that,
They gave him afterward every day, they became part of him.

The mother at home quietly placing the dishes on the supper-table,
The mother with mild words, clean her cap and gown,
    a wholesome odor falling off her person and clothes
    as she walks by,

The father, strong, self-sufficient, manly, mean, angered, unjust,
The blow, the quick loud word, the tight bargain, the crafty lure,
The family usages, the language, the company, the furniture,
   the yearning and swelling heart,
Affection that will not be gainsayed, the sense of what is real,
   the thought if after all it should prove unreal,
The doubts of day-time and the doubts of night-time,
   the curious whether and how,
Whether that which appears so is so,
   or is it all flashes and specks?
Men and women crowding fast in the streets,
   if they are not flashes and specks what are they?

The streets themselves and the façades of houses,
   and goods in the windows,
Vehicles, teams, the heavy-planked wharves,
   the huge crossing at the ferries,
The village on the highland seen from afar at sunset,
   the river between,
Shadows, aureola and mist, the light falling on roofs
   and gables of white or brown two miles off,
The schooner near by sleepily dropping down the tide,
   the little boat slack-towed astern,
The hurrying tumbling waves,
   quick-broken crests, slapping,
The strata of colored clouds,
   the long bar of maroon-tint away solitary by itself,
   the spread of purity it lies motionless in,
The horizon's edge, the flying sea-crow,
   the fragrance of salt marsh and shore mud,
These became part of that child who went forth every day,
   and who now goes, and will always go forth every day.

*. . . became part
of this child.*

Outward sunshine

THE BAREFOOT BOY
JOHN GREENLEAF WHITTIER

Blessings on thee, little man,
Barefoot boy, with cheek of tan!
With thy turned-up pantaloons,
And thy merry whistled tunes;
With thy red lip, redder still
Kissed by strawberries on the hill;
With the sunshine on thy face,
Through thy torn brim's jaunty grace;
From my heart I give thee joy,—
I was once a barefoot boy!

Prince thou art,—the grown-up man
Only is republican.
Let the million-dollared ride!
Barefoot, trudging at his side,
Thou hast more than he can buy
In the reach of ear and eye,—
Outward sunshine, inward joy:
Blessings on thee, barefoot boy!

Cheerily, then, my little man,
Live and laugh, as boyhood can!
Though the flinty slopes be hard,
Stubble-speared the new-mown sward,
Every morn shall lead thee through
Fresh baptisms of the dew;
Every evening from thy feet
Shall the cool wind kiss the heat:
All too soon these feet must hide
In the prison cells of pride,
Lose the freedom of the sod,
Like a colt's for work be shod,
Made to tread the mills of toil,
Up and down in ceaseless moil:
Happy if their track be found
Never on forbidden ground;
Happy if they sink not in
Quick and treacherous sands of sin.
Ah! that thou couldst know thy joy,
Ere it passes, barefoot boy!

My Shadow
ROBERT LOUIS STEVENSON

I have a little shadow
   that goes in and out with me,
And what can be the use of him
   is more than I can see.
He is very, very like me,
   from the heels up to the head;
And I see him jump before me,
   when I jump into bed.
The funniest thing about him
   is the way he likes to grow—
Not at all like proper children,
   which is always very slow;
For he sometimes shoots up taller,
   like an india-rubber ball,
And he sometimes gets so little
   that there's none of him at all.

He hasn't got a notion
   of how children ought to play,
And can only make a fool of me
   in every sort of way.
He stays so close beside me,
   he's a coward you can see;
I'd think shame to stick to nursie
   as that shadow sticks to me!
One morning, very early,
   before the sun was up,
I 'rose and found the shining dew
   on every buttercup;
But my lazy little shadow,
   like an arrant sleepy head,
Had stayed at home behind me
   and was fast asleep in bed.

THE HOUSE BY THE SIDE OF THE ROAD
SAM WALTER FOSS

There are hermit souls that live withdrawn
In the place of their self-content;
There are souls like stars, that dwell apart,
In a fellowless firmament;
There are pioneer souls that blaze their paths
Where highways never ran—
But let me live by the side of the road
And be a friend to man.

Let me live in a house by the side of the road,
Where the race of men go by—
The men who are good and the men who are bad,
As good and as bad as I.
I would not sit in the scorner's seat,
Or hurl the cynic's ban—
Let me live in a house by the side of the road
And be a friend to man.

I see from my house by the side of the road,
By the side of the highway of life,
The men who press with the ardor of hope,
The men who are faint with the strife.
But I turn not away from their smiles nor their tears,
Both parts of an infinite plan—
Let me live in a house by the side of the road
And be a friend to man.

Let me live in my house by the side of the road,
It's here the race of men go by—
They are good, they are bad, they are weak, they are strong,
Wise, foolish—so am I;
Then why should I sit in the scorner's seat,
Or hurl the cynic's ban?
Let me live in my house by the side of the road
And be a friend to man.

...and be a friend to man.

Rock Me to Sleep
Elizabeth Akers Allen

Backward, turn backward, O time, in your flight,
Make me a child again just for to-night!
Mother, come back from the echoless shore,
Take me again to your heart as of yore;
Kiss from my forehead the furrows of care,
Smooth the few silver threads out of my hair;
Over my slumbers your loving watch keep;—
Rock me to sleep, Mother—rock me to sleep!

Backward, flow backward, oh, tide of the years!
I am so weary of toil and of tears—
Toil without recompense, tears all in vain—
Take them, and give me my childhood again!
I have grown weary of dust and decay—
Weary of flinging my soul-wealth away;
Weary of sowing for others to reap;—
Rock me to sleep, Mother—rock me to sleep!

No love like mother-love ever has shone;
No other worship abides and endures—
Faithful, unselfish, and patient like yours:
None like a mother can charm away pain
From the sick soul and the world-weary brain.
Slumber's soft calms o'er my heavy lids creep;—
Rock me to sleep, Mother—rock me to sleep!

Mother, dear Mother, the years have been long
Since I last listened your lullaby song:
Sing, then, and unto my soul it shall seem
Womanhood's years have been only a dream.
Clasped to your heart in a loving embrace,
With your light lashes just sweeping my face,
Never hereafter to wake or to weep;—
Rock me to sleep, Mother—rock me to sleep!

New Friends and Old Friends
Joseph Parry

Make new friends, but keep the old;
Those are silver, these are gold.
New-made friendships, like new wine,
Age will mellow and refine.
Friendships that have stood the test—
Time and change—are surely best;
Brow may wrinkle, hair grow gray;
Friendship never knows decay.
For 'mid old friends, tried and true,
Once more we our youth renew.
But old friends, alas! may die;
New friends must their place supply.
Cherish friendship in your breast—
New is good, but old is best;
Make new friends, but keep the old;
Those are silver, these are gold.

The House and the Road
Josephine Preston Peabody

The little Road says, Go,
The little House says, Stay;
And O, it's bonny here at home,
But I must go away.

The little Road, like me,
Would seek and turn and know;
And forth I must, to learn the things
The little Road would show!

And go I must, my dears,
And journey while I may,
Though heart be sore for the little House
That had no word but Stay.

Maybe, no other way
Your child could ever know
Why a little House would have you stay,
When a little Road says, Go.

My Lost Youth
Henry Wadsworth Longfellow

Often I think of the beautiful town
   That is seated by the sea;
Often in thought go up and down
The pleasant streets of that dear old town,
   And my youth comes back to me.
      And a verse of a Lapland song
      Is haunting my memory still:
      "A boy's will is the wind's will,
And the thoughts of youth are long, long thoughts."

I can see the shadowy lines of its trees,
   And catch, in sudden gleams,
The sheen of the far-surrounding seas,
And islands that were the Hesperides
   Of all my boyish dreams.
      And the burden of that old song,
      It murmurs and whispers still:
      "A boy's will is the wind's will,
And the thoughts of youth are long, long thoughts."

I remember the black wharves and the slips,
   And the sea-tides tossing free;
And Spanish sailors with bearded lips,
And the beauty and mystery of the ships,
   And the magic of the sea.
      And the voice of that wayward song
      Is singing and saying still:
      "A boy's will is the wind's will,
And the thoughts of youth are long, long thoughts."

I remember the sea-fight far away,
   How it thunder'd o'er the tide!
And the dead captains, as they lay
In their graves, o'erlooking the tranquil bay
   Where they in battle died.
      And the sound of that mournful song
      Goes through me with a thrill:
      "A boy's will is the wind's will,
And the thoughts of youth are long, long thoughts."

I can see the breezy dome of groves,
   The shadows of Deering's Woods;
And the friendships old and the early loves
Come back with a Sabbath sound, as of doves
   In quiet neighborhoods.
      And the verse of that sweet old song,
      It flutters and murmurs still:
      "A boy's will is the wind's will,
And the thoughts of youth are long, long thoughts."

There are things of which I may not speak;
   There are dreams that cannot die;
There are thoughts that make the strong heart weak,
And bring a pallor into the cheek,
   And a mist before the eye.
      And the words of that fatal song
      Come over me like a chill:
      "A boy's will is the wind's will,
And the thoughts of youth are long, long thoughts."

Strange to me now are the forms I meet
   When I visit the dear old town;
But the native air is pure and sweet,
And the trees that o'ershadow each well-known street,
   As they balance up and down,
      Are singing the beautiful song,
      Are sighing and whispering still:
      "A boy's will is the wind's will,
And the thoughts of youth are long, long thoughts."

And Deering's Woods are fresh and fair,
   And with joy that is almost pain
My heart goes back to wander there,
And among the dreams of the days that were,
   I find my lost youth again.
      And the strange and beautiful song,
      The groves are repeating it still:
      "A boy's will is the wind's will,
And the thoughts of youth are long, long thoughts."

The Fire of Drift-wood
Henry Wadsworth Longfellow

We sat within the farm-house old,
    Whose windows, looking o'er the bay,
Gave to the sea-breeze damp and cold,
    An easy entrance, night and day.

Not far away we saw the port,
    The strange, old-fashioned, silent town,
The lighthouse, the dismantled fort,
    The wooden houses, quaint and brown.

We sat and talked until the night,
    Descending, filled the little room;
Our faces faded from the sight,
    Our voices only broke the gloom.

We spake of many a vanished scene,
    Of what we once had thought and said,
Of what had been, and might have been,
    And who was changed, and who was dead;

And all that fills the hearts of friends,
    When first they feel, with secret pain,
Their lives thenceforth have separate ends,
    And never can be one again;

The first slight swerving of the heart,
    That words are powerless to express,
And leave it still unsaid in part,
    Or say it in too great excess.

The very tones in which we spake
    Had something strange, I could but mark;
The leaves of memory seemed to make
    A mournful rustling in the dark.

Oft died the words upon our lips,
    As suddenly, from out the fire
Built of the wreck of stranded ships,
    The flames would leap and then expire.

And, as their splendor flashed and failed,
    We thought of wrecks upon the main,
Of ships dismasted, that were hailed
    And sent no answer back again.

The windows, rattling in their frames,
    The ocean, roaring up the beach,
The gusty blast, the bickering flames,
    All mingled vaguely in our speech;

Until they made themselves a part
    Of fancies floating through the brain,
The long-lost ventures of the heart,
    That send no answers back again.

O flames that glowed! O hearts that yearned!
    They were indeed too much akin,
The drift-wood fire without that burned,
    The thoughts that burned and glowed within.

My Mother's Hands
AUTHOR UNKNOWN

Such beautiful, beautiful hands!
    They're neither white nor small;
And you, I know, would scarcely think
    That they were fair at all.
I've looked on hands whose form and hue
    A sculptor's dream might be;
Yet are those wrinkled, aged hands
    Most beautiful to me.

Such beautiful, beautiful hands!
    Though heart were weary and sad,
These patient hands kept toiling on,
    That the children might be glad;
I always weep, as looking back
    To childhood's distant day,
I think how those hands rested not,
    When mine were at their play.

Such beautiful, beautiful hands!
    They're growing feeble now,
For time and pain have left their mark
    On hands, and heart, and brow.
Alas! alas! the nearing time,
    And the sad, sad day to me,
When 'neath the daisies, out of sight,
    These hands will folded be.

But oh, beyond this shadow land,
    Where all is bright and fair,
I know full well these dear old hands
    Will palms of victory bear;
Where crystal streams through endless years
    Flow over golden sands,
And where the old grow young again,
    I'll clasp my mother's hands.

My Mother
JANE TAYLOR

Who fed me from her gentle breast
And hushed me in her arms to rest,
And on my cheek sweet kisses prest?
    My mother.

When sleep forsook my open eye,
Who was it sung sweet lullaby
And rocked me that I should not cry?
    My mother.

Who sat and watched my infant head
When sleeping in my cradle bed,
And tears of sweet affection shed?
    My mother.

Who taught my infant lips to pray,
To love God's holy word and day,
And walk in wisdom's pleasant way?
    My mother.

And can I ever cease to be
Affectionate and kind to thee
Who wast so very kind to me,—
    My mother.

Oh no, the thought I cannot bear;
And if God please my life to spare
I hope I shall reward thy care,
    My mother.

When thou art feeble, old and gray,
My healthy arm shall be thy stay,
And I will soothe thy pains away,
    My mother.

And when I see thee hang thy head,
'Twill be my turn to watch thy bed,
And tears of sweet affection shed,—
    My mother.

GRANDFATHER'S CLOCK
HENRY CLAY WORK

My grandfather's clock was too large for the shelf,
    So it stood ninety years on the floor;
It was taller by half than the old man himself,
    Though it weighed not a pennyweight more.
It was bought on the morn of the day that he was born
    And was always his treasure and pride.
But it stopped short—never to go again—
    When the old man died.

Ninety years without slumbering
    Tick, tick, tick, tick.
His life-seconds numbering
    Tick, tick, tick, tick.
It stopped short—never to go again—
    When the old man died.

In watching its pendulum swing to and fro
    Many hours had he spent while a boy;
And in childhood and manhood the clock seemed to know
    And to share both his grief and his joy,
For it struck twenty-four when he entered the door
    With a blooming and beautiful bride,
But it stopped short—never to go again—
    When the old man died.

It rang an alarm in the dead of night—
    An alarm that for years had been dumb.
And we knew that his spirit was pluming for flight
    That his hour for departure had come.
Still the clock kept the time with a soft and muffled chime
    As we silently stood by his side;
But it stopped short—never to go again—
    When the old man died.

Light

FROM OLD SUPERSTITIONS
AUTHOR UNKNOWN

See a pin and pick it up,
All the day you'll have good luck.
See a pin and let it lay,
Bad luck you will have all day.
The maid who, on the first of May,
Goes to the fields at break of day,
And washes in dew from the hawthorn tree,
Will ever after handsome be.
Friday night's dream on a Saturday told,

Verse

Is sure to come true, be it never so old.
Monday's child is fair of face,
Tuesday's child is full of grace,
Wednesday's child is full of woe,
Thursday's child has far to go,
Friday's child is loving and giving,

Saturday's child works hard for its living,
And a child that is born on the Sabbath day
Is fair and wise and good and gay.

THE TABLE AND THE CHAIR
EDWARD LEAR

Said the Table to the Chair,
"You can hardly be aware
How I suffer from the heat
And from chilblains on my feet.

"If we took a little walk,
We might have a little talk;
Pray let us take the air,"
Said the Table to the Chair.

Said the Chair unto the Table,
"Now you *know* we are not able:
How foolishly you talk,
When you know we *cannot* walk!"

Said the Table with a sigh,
"It can do no harm to try.
I've as many legs as you:
Why can't we walk on two?"

So they both went slowly down,
And walked about the town
With a cheerful bumpy sound
And they toddled round and round;

And everybody cried,
As they hastened to their side,
"See! the Table and the Chair
Have come out to take the air!"

But in going down an alley
To a castle in the valley
They completely lost their way,
And wandered all the day;

Till to see them safely back,
They paid a Ducky-quack,
And a beetle, and a Mouse,
Who took them to their house.

What a lovely walk . . .

The Spider and the Fly
Mary Howitt

"Will you walk into my parlor?" said the Spider to the Fly,
"'Tis the prettiest little parlor that ever you did spy;
The way into my parlor is up a winding stair,
And I have many curious things to show when you are there."
"Oh no, no," said the little Fly, "to ask me is in vain;
For who goes up your winding stair can ne'er come down again."

Said the cunning Spider to the Fly, "Dear friend, what can I do
To prove the warm affection I've always felt for you?
I have within my pantry, good store of all that's nice;
I'm sure you're very welcome—will you please to take a slice?"
"Oh no, no," said the little Fly, "kind sir, that cannot be,
I've heard what's in your pantry, and I do not wish to see!"

The Spider turned him round about, and went into his den,
For well he knew the silly Fly would soon be back again;
So he wove a subtle web in a little corner sly,
And set his table ready to dine upon the Fly.
Then he came out to his door again, and merrily did sing,
"Come hither, hither, pretty Fly, with the pearl and silver wing;
Your robes are green and purple, there's a crest upon your head;
Your eyes are like the diamond bright, but mine are dull as lead."

Alas, alas! how very soon this silly little Fly,
Hearing his wily, flattering words, came slowly flitting by;
With buzzing wings she hung aloft, then near and nearer drew,—
Thinking only of her brilliant eyes, and green and purple hue;
Thinking only of her crested head—poor foolish thing! At last,
Up jumped the cunning Spider, and fiercely held her fast.
He dragged her up his winding stair, into his dismal den
Within his little parlor—but she ne'er came out again!

And now, dear little children, who may this story read,
To idle, silly, flattering words, I pray you ne'er give heed;
Unto an evil counsellor close heart, and ear, and eye,
And take a lesson from this tale of the Spider and the Fly.

THE WALRUS AND THE CARPENTER
LEWIS CARROLL

"O Oysters, come and walk with us!"
   The Walrus did beseech.
"A pleasant walk, a pleasant talk,
   Along the briny beach:
We cannot do with more than four,
   To give a hand to each."

The eldest Oyster looked at him,
   But never a word he said:
The eldest Oyster winked his eye,
   And shook his heavy head—
Meaning to say he did not choose
   To leave the oyster-bed.

But four young Oysters hurried up,
   All eager for the treat:
Their coats were brushed, their faces washed,
   Their shoes were clean and neat—
And this was odd, because, you know,
   They hadn't any feet.

Four other Oysters followed them,
   And yet another four;
And thick and fast they came at last,
   And more, and more, and more—
All hopping through the frothy waves,
   And scrambling to the shore.

The Walrus and the Carpenter
   Walked on a mile or so,
And then they rested on a rock
   Conveniently low:
And all the little Oysters stood
   And waited in a row.

"The time has come," the Walrus said,
   "To talk of many things:
Of shoes—and ships—and sealing wax—
   Of cabbages—and kings—
And why the sea is boiling hot—
   And whether pigs have wings."

"A loaf of bread," the Walrus said,
   "Is what we chiefly need:
Pepper and vinegar besides
   Are very good indeed—
Now, if you're ready, Oysters dear,
   We can begin to feed."

"But not on us!" the Oysters cried,
   Turning a little blue.
"After such kindness, that would be
   A dismal thing to do!"
"The night is fine," the Walrus said,
   "Do you admire the view?

"It seems a shame," the Walrus said,
   "To play them such a trick.
After we've brought them out so far,
   And made them trot so quick!"
The Carpenter said nothing but
   "The butter's spread too thick!"

"O Oysters," said the Carpenter,
   "You've had a pleasant run!
Shall we be trotting home again?"
   But answer came there none—
And this was scarcely odd, because
   They'd eaten every one.

THE DUEL
EUGENE FIELD

The gingham dog and the calico cat
Side by side on the table sat;
'Twas half past twelve, and (what do you think!)
Nor one nor t'other had slept a wink!
    The old Dutch clock and the Chinese plate
    Appeared to know as sure as fate
There was going to be a terrible spat.
        (I wasn't there; I simply state
        What was told to me by the Chinese plate!)
The gingham dog went "Bow-wow-wow!"
And the calico cat replied "Mee-ow!"
The air was littered, an hour or so,
With bits of gingham and calico,
    While the old Dutch clock in the chimney place
    Up with its hands before its face,
For it always dreaded a family row!
        (Now mind: I'm only telling you
        What the old Dutch clock declares is true!)

The Chinese plate looked very blue,
And wailed, "Oh, dear! what shall we do!"
But the gingham dog and the calico cat
Wallowed this way and tumbled that,
    Employing every tooth and claw
    In the awfullest way you ever saw—
And, oh! how the gingham and calico flew!
        (Don't fancy I exaggerate—
        I got my news from the Chinese plate!)
Next morning where the two had sat
They found no trace of dog or cat:
And some folks think unto this day
That burglars stole that pair away!
    But the truth about the cat and pup
    Is this: they ate each other up!
Now what do you really think of that!
        (The old Dutch clock it told me so,
        And that is how I came to know.)

JABBERWOCKY
LEWIS CARROLL

'Twas brillig, and the slithy toves
    Did gyre and gimble in the wabe;
All mimsy were the borogoves,
    And the mome raths outgrabe.

"Beware the Jabberwock, my son!
    The jaws that bite, the claws that catch!
Beware the Jubjub bird, and shun
    The frumious Bandersnatch!"

He took his vorpal sword in hand:
    Long time the manxome foe he sought—
So rested he by the Tumtum tree,
    And stood awhile in thought.

And as in uffish thought he stood,
    The Jabberwock, with eyes of flame,
Came whiffling through the tulgey wood,
    And burbled as it came!

One, two! One, two! And through and through
    The vorpal blade went snicker-snack!
He left it dead, and with its head
    He went galumphing back.

"And hast thou slain the Jabberwock?
    Come to my arms, my beamish boy!
O frabjous day! Callooh! Callay!"
    He chortled in his joy.

'Twas brillig, and the slithy toves
    Did gyre and gimble in the wabe;
All mimsy were the borogoves,
    And the mome raths outgrabe.

So rested he by the Tumtum tree . . .

THE TALE OF CUSTARD THE DRAGON
OGDEN NASH

Belinda lived in a little white house,
With a little black kitten and a little grey mouse,
And a little yellow dog and a little red wagon,
And a realio, trulio, little pet dragon.

Now the name of the little black kitten was Ink,
And the little grey mouse, she called her Blink,
And the little yellow dog was sharp as Mustard,
But the dragon was a coward, and she called him Custard.

Custard the dragon had big sharp teeth,
And spikes on top of him and scales underneath,
Mouth like a fireplace, chimney for a nose,
And realio, trulio daggers on his toes.

Belinda was as brave as a barrelful of bears,
And Ink and Blink chased lions down the stairs,
Mustard was as brave as a tiger in a rage,
But Custard cried for a nice safe cage.

Belinda tickled him, she tickled him unmerciful,
Ink, Blink and Mustard, they rudely called him Percival,
They all sat laughing in the little red wagon
At the realio, trulio, cowardly dragon.

Belinda giggled till she shook the house,
And Blink said *Weeek!*, which is giggling for a mouse,
Ink and Mustard rudely asked his age,
When Custard cried for a nice safe cage.

Suddenly, suddenly they heard a nasty sound,
And Mustard growled, and they all looked around.
Meowch! cried Ink, and Ooh! cried Belinda,
For there was a pirate, climbing in the winda.

Pistol in his left hand, pistol in his right,
And he held in his teeth a cutlass bright;
His beard was black, one leg was wood.
It was clear that the pirate meant no good.

Belinda paled, and she cried Help! Help!
But Mustard fled with a terrified yelp,
Ink trickled down to the bottom of the household,
And little mouse Blink strategically mouseholed.

But up jumped Custard, snorting like an engine,
Clashed his tail like irons in a dungeon,
With a clatter and a clank and a jangling squirm
He went at the pirate like a robin at a worm.

The pirate gaped at Belinda's dragon,
And gulped some grog from his pocket flagon,
He fired two bullets, but they didn't hit,
And Custard gobbled him, every bit.

Belinda embraced him, Mustard licked him;
No one mourned for his pirate victim.
Ink and Blink in glee did gyrate
Around the dragon that ate the pyrate.

Belinda still lives in her little white house,
With her little black kitten and her little grey mouse,
And her little yellow dog and her little red wagon,
And her realio, trulio, little pet dragon.

Belinda is as brave as a barrelful of bears,
And Ink and Blink chase lions down the stairs,
Mustard is as brave as a tiger in a rage,
But Custard keeps crying for a nice safe cage.

We set around the kitchen

LITTLE ORPHANT ANNIE
JAMES WHITCOMB RILEY

Little Orphant Annie's come to our house to stay,
An' wash the cups and saucers up, and brush the crumbs away,
An' shoo the chickens off the porch, an' dust the hearth, an' sweep,
An' make the fire, an' bake the bread, an' earn her board-an'-keep;
An' all us other children, when the supper things is done,
We set around the kitchen fire an' has the mostest fun
A-list'nin' to the witch-tales 'at Annie tells about,
An' the Gobble-uns 'at gits you

    Ef you
        Don't
            Watch
                Out!

Onc't they was a little boy wouldn't say his pray'rs—
An' when he went to bed at night, away up stairs,
His mammy heerd him holler, an' his daddy heerd him bawl,
An' when they turn't the kivvers down, he wasn't there at all!
An' they seeked him in the rafter-room, an' cubby-hole, an' press.
An' seeked him up the chimbly-flue, an' ever'wheres, I guess;
But all they ever found was thist his pants an' roundabout!
An' the Gobble-uns 'll git you

    Ef you
        Don't
            Watch
                Out!

fire an' has the mostest fun

An' one time a little girl 'ud allus laugh an' grin,
An' make fun of ever' one, an' all her blood-an'-kin;
An' onc't when they was "company," an' ole folks was there,
She mocked 'em an' shocked 'em, an' said she didn't care!
An' thist as she kicked her heels, an' turn't to run an' hide,
They was two great big Black Things a-standin' by her side,
An' they snatched her through the ceilin' 'fore she knowed what she's about!
An' the Gobble-uns 'll git you

    Ef you

        Don't

            Watch

                Out!

An' little Orphant Annie says, when the blaze is blue,
An' the lampwick sputters, an' the wind goes woo-oo!
An' you hear the crickets quit, an' the moon is gray,
An' the lightnin' bugs in dew is all squenched away,—
You better mind yer parents, and yer teachers fond and dear,
An' churish them 'at loves you, an' dry the orphant's tear,
An' help the pore an' needy ones 'at clusters all about,
Er the Gobble-uns 'll git you

    Ef you

        Don't

            Watch

                Out!

THE BELLS
EDGAR ALLAN POE

Hear the sledges with the bells—
    Silver bells!
What a world of merriment their melody foretells!
  How they tinkle, tinkle, tinkle,
    In the icy air of night!
  While the stars that oversprinkle
  All the heavens, seem to twinkle
    With a crystalline delight;
  Keeping time, time, time,
    In a sort of Runic rhyme,
To the tintinnabulation that so musically wells
  From the bells, bells, bells, bells,
    Bells, bells, bells—
From the jingling and the tinkling of the bells.

II

  Hear the mellow wedding bells—
    Golden bells!
What a world of happiness their harmony foretells!
    Through the balmy air of night
  How they ring out their delight!—
    From the molten-golden notes,
      And all in tune,
    What a liquid ditty floats
To the turtle-dove that listens, while she gloats
    On the moon!
  Oh, from out the sounding cells,
What a gush of euphony voluminously wells!
    How it swells!
    How it dwells
    On the Future!—how it tells
    Of the rapture that impels
    To the swinging and the ringing
    Of the bells, bells, bells—
    Of the bells, bells, bells, bells,
      Bells, bells, bells—
To the rhyming and the chiming of the bells!

III

  Hear the loud alarum bells—
    Brazen bells!
What a tale of terror, now their turbulency tells!
  In the startled ear of night
  How they scream out their affright!
    Too much horrified to speak,
    They can only shriek, shriek,
      Out of tune,
In a clamorous appealing to the mercy of the fire,
In a mad expostulation with the deaf and frantic fire,
    Leaping higher, higher, higher,
    With a desperate desire,
    And a resolute endeavor
    Now—Now to sit, or never,
By the side of the pale-faced moon.
    Oh, the bells, bells, bells!
    What a tale their terror tells
    Of Despair!
How they clang, and clash, and roar!
What a horror they outpour
On the bosom of the palpitating air!
    Yet the ear, it fully knows,
      By the twanging,
      And the clanging,
    How the danger ebbs and flows;
    Yet the ear distinctly tells,
      In the jangling,
      And the wrangling,
    How the danger sinks and swells,
By the sinking or the swelling in the anger of the bells—
      Of the bells—
    Of the bells, bells, bells, bells,
      Bells, bells, bells—
In the clamor and the clanging of the bells!

IV

  Hear the tolling of the bells—
    Iron bells!
What a world of solemn thought their monody compels!

In the silence of the night,
How we shiver with affright
At the melancholy menace of their tone!
For every sound that floats
From the rust within their throats
Is a groan.
And the people—ah, the people—
They that dwell up in the steeple,
All alone,
And who, tolling, tolling, tolling,
In that muffled monotone,
Feel a glory in so rolling
On the human heart a stone—
They are neither man nor woman—
They are neither brute nor human—
They are Ghouls:—
And their king it is who tolls:—
And he rolls, rolls, rolls,
Rolls
A pæan from the bells!
And his merry bosom swells
With the pæan of the bells!
And he dances, and he yells;
Keeping time, time, time,
In a sort of Runic rhyme,
To the pæan of the bells:—
Of the bells:
Keeping time, time, time,
In a sort of Runic rhyme,
To the throbbing of the bells:—
Of the bells, bells, bells—
To the sobbing of the bells:—
Keeping time, time, time,
As he knells, knells, knells,
In a happy Runic rhyme,
To the rolling of the bells—
Of the bells, bells, bells:—
To the tolling of the bells—
Of the bells, bells, bells, bells,
Bells, bells, bells—
To the moaning and the groaning of the bells.

A world of
merriment . . .

And you shall see

THE LAST LEAF
OLIVER WENDELL HOLMES

I saw him once before,
As he passed by the door,
   And again
The pavement stones resound
As he totters o'er the ground
   With his cane.

They say that in his prime
Ere the pruning-knife of Time
   Cut him down,
Not a better man was found
By the Crier on his round
   Through the town.

But now he walks the streets,
And looks at all he meets
   Sad and wan,
And he shakes his feeble head,
That it seems as if he said,
   "They are gone."

The mossy marbles rest
On the lips that he has prest
   In their bloom,
And the names he loved to hear
Have been carved for many a year
   On the tomb.

My grandmama has said,—
Poor old lady, she is dead
   Long ago,—
That he had a Roman nose,
And his cheek was like a rose
   In the snow.

But now his nose is thin,
And it rests upon his chin
   Like a staff,
And a crook is in his back,
And a melancholy crack
   In his laugh.

I know it is a sin
For me to sit and grin
   At him here;
But the old three-cornered hat,
And the breeches, and all that,
   Are so queer!

And if I should live to be
The last leaf upon the tree
   In the spring,—
Let them smile, as I do now,
At the old forsaken bough
   Where I cling.

the beautiful things

WYNKEN, BLYNKEN, AND NOD
Eugene Field

Wynken, Blynken, and Nod one night
    Sailed off in a wooden shoe—
Sailed on a river of crystal light
    Into a sea of dew.
"Where are you going, and what do you wish?"
    The old moon asked the three.
"We have come to fish for the herring-fish
    That live in this beautiful sea;
    Nets of silver and gold have we,"
       Said Wynken,
       Blynken,
       And Nod.

The old moon laughed and sang a song,
    As they rocked in the wooden shoe;
And the wind that sped them all night long
    Ruffled the waves of dew;
The little stars were the herring-fish
    That lived in the beautiful sea.
"Now cast your nets wherever you wish—
    Never afeard are we!"
    So cried the stars to the fishermen three,
       Wynken,
       Blynken,
       And Nod.

All night long their nets they threw
    To the stars in the twinkling foam—
Then down from the skies came the wooden shoe,
    Bringing the fishermen home:
'Twas all so pretty a sail, it seemed
    As if it could not be;
And some folk thought 'twas a dream they'd dreamed
    Of sailing that beautiful sea;
    But I shall name you the fishermen three:
       Wynken,
       Blynken,
       And Nod.

Wynken and Blynken are two little eyes,
    And Nod is a little head,
And the wooden shoe that sailed the skies
    Is a wee one's trundle-bed;
So shut your eyes while Mother sings
    Of wonderful sights that be,
And you shall see the beautiful things
    As you rock on the misty sea
    Where the old shoe rocked the fishermen three,—
       Wynken,
       Blynken,
       And Nod.

CATALOGUE
ROSALIE MOORE

Cats sleep fat and walk thin.
Cats, when they sleep, slump;
When they wake, stretch and begin
Over, pulling their ribs in.
Cats walk thin.

Cats wait in a lump,
Jump in a streak.
Cats, when they jump, are sleek
As a grape slipping its skin—
They have technique.
Oh, cats don't creak.
They sneak.

Cats sleep fat.
They spread out comfort underneath them
Like a good mat,
As if they picked the place
And then sat.
You walk around one
As if he were the city hall
After that.

A cat condenses.
He pulls in his tail to go under bridges,
And himself to go under fences.
Cats fit
In any size box or kit;
And if a large pumpkin grew under one,
He could arch over it.

When everyone else is just ready to go out,
The cat is just ready to come in.
He's not where he's been.
Cats sleep fat and walk thin.

I HAD A HIPPOPOTAMUS
PATRICK BARRINGTON

I had a hippopotamus; I kept him in a shed
And fed him upon vitamins and vegetable bread;
I made him my companion on many cheery walks
And had his portrait done by a celebrity in chalks.

His charming eccentricities were known on every side,
The creature's popularity was wonderfully wide;
He frolicked with the Rector in a dozen friendly tussles,
Who could not but remark upon his hippopotamuscles.

If he should be afflicted by depression or the dumps,
By hippopotameasles or the hippopotamumps,
I never knew a particle of peace till it was plain
He was hippopotamasticating properly again.

I had a hippopotamus; I loved him as a friend;
But beautiful relationships are bound to have an end.
Time takes, alas! our joys from us and robs us of our blisses;
My hippopotamus turned out a hippopotamissis.

My housekeeper regarded him with jaundice in her eye;
She did not want a colony of hippopotami;
She borrowed a machine-gun from her soldier-nephew, Percy,
And showed my hippopotamus no hippopotamercy.

My house now lacks the glamour that the charming creature gave,
The garage where I kept him is as silent as the grave;
No longer he displays among the motor-tyres and spanners
His hippopotamastery of hippopotamanners.

No longer now he gambols in the orchard in the Spring
No longer do I lead him through the village on a string;
No longer in the mornings does the neighbourhood rejoice
To his hippopotamusically-modulated voice.

I had a hippopotamus; but nothing upon earth
Is constant in its happiness or lasting in its mirth.
No joy that life can give me can be strong enough to smother
My sorrow for that might-have-been-a-hippopotamother.

MR. NOBODY
AUTHOR UNKNOWN

I know a funny little man,
    As quiet as a mouse.
He does the mischief that is done
    In everybody's house.
Though no one ever sees his face,
    Yet one and all agree
That every plate we break, was cracked
    By Mr. Nobody.

'Tis he who always tears our books,
    Who leaves the door ajar.
He picks the buttons from our shirts,
    And scatters pins afar.
That squeaking door will always squeak—
    For prithee, don't you see?
We leave the oiling to be done
    By Mr. Nobody.

He puts damp wood upon the fire,
    That kettles will not boil:
His are the feet that bring in mud
    And all the carpets soil.
The papers that so oft are lost—
    Who had them last but he?
There's no one tosses them about
    But Mr. Nobody.

The fingermarks upon the door
    By none of us were made.
We never leave the blinds unclosed
    To let the curtains fade.
The ink we never spill! The boots
    That lying round you see,
Are not our boots—they all belong
    To Mr. Nobody.

He does the mischief

FROM SONG OF THE OPEN ROAD
WALT WHITMAN

Afoot and light-hearted, I take to the open road,
Healthy, free, the world before me,
The long brown path before me, leading wherever I choose.

Henceforth I ask not good fortune—I myself am good-fortune;
Henceforth I whimper no more, postpone no more, need nothing,
Strong and content, I travel the open road. . . .

From this hour, freedom!
From this hour I ordain myself loos'd of limits and imaginary lines,
Going where I list, my own master, total and absolute,
Listening to others, and considering well what they say,
Pausing, searching, receiving, contemplating,
Gently, but with undeniable will, divesting myself,
    of the holds that would hold me.

I am larger, better than I thought;
I did not know I held so much goodness.
All seems beautiful to me;
I can repeat over to men and women, You have done such good to me,
    I would do the same to you.

I will recruit for myself and you as I go;
I will scatter myself among men and women as I go;
I will toss the new gladness and roughness among them;
Whoever denies me, it shall not trouble me;
Whoever accepts me, he or she shall be blessed, and shall bless me. . . .

Allons! be not detain'd!
Let the papers remain on the desk unwritten,
    and the book on the shelf unopen'd!

Let the tools remain in the workshop! let the money remain unearn'd!
Let the school stand! mind not the cry of the teacher!
Let the preacher preach in the pulpit! let the lawyer plead in the court,
    and the judge expound the law.

Mon enfant! I give you my hand!
I give you my love, more precious than money,
I give you myself, before preaching or law:
Will you give me yourself? will you come travel with me?
Shall we stick by each other as long as we live?

WHEN THE FROST IS ON THE PUNKIN
JAMES WHITCOMB RILEY

When the frost is on the punkin and the fodder's in the shock,
And you hear the kyouck and gobble of the struttin' turkey-cock,
And the clackin' of the guineys, and the cluckin' of the hens,
And the rooster's hallylooer as he tiptoes on the fence;
Oh, it's then's the times a feller is a-feelin' at his best,
With the risin' sun to greet him from a night of peaceful rest,
As he leaves the house, bareheaded, and goes out to feed the stock,
When the frost is on the punkin and the fodder's in the shock.

They's something kind o' harty-like about the atmusfere
When the heat of summer's over and the coolin' fall is here.—
Of course we miss the flowers, and the blossoms on the trees,
And the mumble of the hummin'-birds and buzzin' of the bees;
But the air's so appetizin', and the landscape through the haze
Of a crisp and sunny morning of the airly autumn days
Is a pictur' that no painter has the colorin' to mock,—
When the frost is on the punkin and the fodder's in the shock.

The husky, rusty russel of the tossels of the corn,
And the raspin' of the tangled leaves, as golden as the morn;
The stubble in the furries—kind o' lonesome-like, but still
A-preachin' sermuns to us of the barns they growed to fill;
The straw-stack in the medder, and the reaper in the shed;
The hosses in theyr stalls below, the clover overhead,—
Oh, it sets my hart a-clickin' like the tickin' of a clock,
When the frost is on the punkin and the fodder's in the shock!

Then your apples all is gethered, and the ones a feller keeps
Is poured around the cellar-floor in red and yaller heaps;
And your cider-makin' 's over, and your wimmern-folks is through
With their mince and apple butter, and theyr souse and sausage, too!—
I don't know how to tell it—but ef sich a thing could be
As the Angels wantin' boardin', and they'd call around on *me*—
I'd want to 'commodate 'em—all the whole-indurin' flock—
When the frost is on the punkin and the fodder's in the shock!

*Afoot and light-hearted,
I take to the open road.*

My Dog

John Kendrick Bangs

I have no dog, but it must be
Somewhere there's one belongs to me—
A little chap with wagging tail,
And dark brown eyes that never quail,
But look you through, and through, and through,
With love unspeakable and true.

Somewhere it must be, I opine,
There is a little dog of mine
With cold black nose that sniffs around
In search of what things may be found
In pocket or some nook hard by
Where I have hid them from his eye.

Somewhere my doggie pulls and tugs
The fringes of rebellious rugs,
Or with the mischief of the pup
Chews all my shoes and slippers up,
And when he's done it to the core,
With eyes all eager, pleads for more.

Somewhere upon his hinder legs
My little doggie sits and begs,
And in a wistful minor tone
Pleads for the pleasures of the bone—
I pray it be his owner's whim
To yield, and grant the same to him.

Somewhere a little dog doth wait;
It may be by some garden gate.
With eyes alert and tail attent—
You know the kind of tail that's meant—
With stores of yelps of glad delight
To bid me welcome home at night.

Somewhere a little dog is seen,
His nose two shaggy paws between,
Flat on his stomach, one eye shut
Held fast in dreamy slumber, but
The other open, ready for
His master coming through the door.

I Am the Cat
Leila Usher

In Egypt they worshiped me—
    I am the Cat.
Because I bend not to the will of man
    They call me a mystery.
When I catch and play with a mouse,
    They call me cruel,
Yet they take animals to keep
    In parks and zoos, that they may gape at them.
They think all animals are made for their pleasure,
    To be their slaves.
And, while I kill only for my needs,
    They kill for pleasure, power and gold,
And then pretend to a superiority!
    Why should I love them?
I, the Cat, whose ancestors
    Proudly trod the jungle,
Not one ever tamed by man.
    Ah, do they know
That the same immortal hand
    That gave them breath, gave breath to me?
But I alone am free—
    I am THE CAT.

I Think I Know No Finer Things Than Dogs
Hally Carrington Brent

Though prejudice perhaps my mind befogs,
I think I know no finer things than dogs:
The young ones, they of gay and bounding heart,
Who lure us in their games to take a part,
Who with mock tragedy their antics cloak
And, from their wild eyes' tail, admit the joke;
The old ones, with their wistful, fading eyes,
They who desire no further paradise

Little Lost Pup
Arthur Guiterman

He was lost!—not a shade of doubt of that;
For he never barked at a slinking cat,
But stood in the square where the wind blew raw
With a drooping ear and a trembling paw
And a mournful look in his pleading eye
And a plaintive sniff at the passer-by
That begged as plain as a tongue could sue,
"O Mister! please may I follow you?"
A lorn wee waif of a tawny brown
Adrift in the roar of a heedless town.
Oh, the saddest of sights in a world of sin
Is a little lost pup with his tail tucked in!

Now he shares my board and he owns my bed,
And he fairly shouts when he hears my tread;
Then, if things go wrong, as they sometimes do,
And the world is cold and I'm feeling blue,
He asserts his right to assuage my woes
With a warm, red tongue and a nice, cold nose
And a silky head on my arm or knee
And a paw as soft as a paw can be.

When we rove the woods for a league about
He's as full of pranks as a school let out;
For he romps and frisks like a three months' colt,
And he runs me down like a thunderbolt.
Oh, the blithest of sights in the world so fair
Is a gay little pup with his tail in the air!

Than the warm comfort of our smile and hand,
Who tune their moods to ours and understand
Each word and gesture; they who lie and wait
To welcome us—with no rebuke if late.
Sublime the love they bear; but ask to live
Close to our feet, unrecompensed to give;
Beside which many men seem very logs—
I think I know no finer things than dogs.

HOW DO I LOVE THEE?
FROM SONNETS FROM THE PORTUGUESE
ELIZABETH BARRETT BROWNING

How do I love thee? Let me count the ways.

I love thee to the depth and breadth and height
My soul can reach, when feeling out of sight
For the ends of Being and ideal Grace.
I love thee to the level of every day's
Most quiet need, by sun and candle-light.

of Love

I love thee freely, as men strive for Right;
I love thee purely, as men turn from Praise.
I love thee with the passion put to use
In my old griefs, and with my childhood's faith.
I love thee with a love I seemed to lose

With my lost saints,—I love thee with the breath,
Smiles, tears, of all my life!—and, if God choose,
I shall but love thee better after death.

I Taste a Liquor Never Brewed
Emily Dickinson

I taste a liquor never brewed,
From tankards scooped in pearl;
Not all the vats upon the Rhine
Yield such an alcohol!

Inebriate of air am I,
And debauchee of dew,
Reeling, through endless summer days,
From inns of molten blue.

When landlords turn the drunken bee
Out of the foxglove's door,
When butterflies renounce their dreams,
I shall but drink the more!

Till seraphs swing their snowy hats,
And saints to windows run,
To see the little tippler
Leaning against the sun!

Shall I Compare Thee to a Summer's Day?
William Shakespeare

Shall I compare thee to a summer's day?
Thou art more lovely and more temperate:
Rough winds do shake the darling buds of May,
And summer's lease hath all too short a date:
Sometimes too hot the eye of heaven shines,
And every fair form from fair sometimes declines,
By chance or nature's changing course untrimm'd;
But thy eternal summer shall not fade,
Nor lose possession of that fair thou owest;
Nor shall Death brag thou wander'st in his shade,
When in eternal lines to time thou grow'st:
    So long as men can breathe, or eyes can see,
    So long lives this, and this gives life to thee.

When I Was One-and-Twenty
A. E. Housman

When I was one-and-twenty
    I heard a wise man say,
"Give crowns and pounds and guineas
    But not your heart away;
Give pearls away and rubies
    But keep your fancy free."
But I was one-and-twenty,
    No use to talk to me.

When I was one-and-twenty
    I heard him say again,
"The heart out of the bosom
    Was never given in vain;
'Tis paid with sighs a-plenty
    And sold for endless rue."
And I am two-and-twenty,
    And oh, 'tis true, 'tis true.

A Red, Red Rose
Robert Burns

O, my luve is like a red, red rose,
    That's newly sprung in June.
O, my luve is like the melodie,
    That's sweetly play'd in tune.

As fair art thou, my bonie lass,
    So deep in luve am I,
And I will luve thee still, my dear,
    Till a' the seas gang dry.

Till a' the seas gang dry, my dear,
    And the rocks melt wi' the sun!
And I will luve thee still, my dear,
    While the sands o' life shall run.

And fare thee weel, my only luve,
    And fare thee weel a while!
And I will come again, my luve,
    Tho' it were ten thousand mile!

She Walks in Beauty
George Gordon, Lord Byron

She walks in beauty like the night
  Of cloudless climes and starry skies;
And all that's best of dark and bright
  Meets in her aspect and her eyes:
Thus mellow'd to that tender light
  Which heaven to gaudy day denies.

One shade the more, one ray the less,
  Had half impair'd the nameless grace
Which waves in every raven tress,
  Or softly lightens o'er her face—
Where thoughts serenely sweet express
  How pure, how dear their dwelling-place.

And on that cheek, and o'er that brow,
  So soft, so calm, yet eloquent,
The smiles that win, the tints that glow,
  But tell of days in goodness spent,
A mind at peace with all below,
  A heart whose love is innocent.

Jenny Kissed Me
James Henry Leigh Hunt

Jenny kissed me when we met,
  Jumping from the chair she sat in.
Time, you thief! who love to get
  Sweets into your list, put that in.
Say I'm weary, say I'm sad;
  Say that health and wealth have missed me;
Say I'm growing old, but add—
  Jenny kissed me!

*My love is like
a red, red rose.*

THE LADY OF SHALOTT
ALFRED, LORD TENNYSON

Part One

Willows whiten, aspens quiver,
Little breezes dusk and shiver
Thro' the wave that runs for ever
By the island in the river
 Flowing down to Camelot.
Four gray walls, and four gray towers,
Overlook a space of flowers,
And the silent isle imbowers
 The Lady of Shalott.

By the margin, willow-veil'd,
Slide the heavy barges trail'd
By slow horses; and unhail'd
The shallop flitteth silken-sail'd
 Skimming down to Camelot:
But who hath seen her wave her hand?
Or at the casement seen her stand?
Or is she known in all the land,
 The Lady of Shalott?

Only reapers, reaping early
In among the bearded barley,
Hear a song that echoes cheerly
From the river winding clearly,
 Down to tower'd Camelot;
And by the moon the reaper weary,
Piling sheaves in uplands airy,
Listening, whispers "'Tis the fairy
 Lady of Shalott."

Part Two

There she weaves by night and day
A magic web with colors gay.
She has heard a whisper say,
A curse is on her if she stay
 To look down to Camelot.
She knows not what the curse may be,

And so she weaveth steadily,
And little other care hath she,
 The Lady of Shalott.

And moving thro' a mirror clear
That hangs before her all the year,
Shadows of the world appear.
There she sees the highway near
 Winding down to Camelot;
There the river eddy whirls,
And there the surly village-churls,
And the red cloaks of market girls,
 Pass onward from Shalott.

Sometimes a troop of damsels glad,
Or an abbot or an ambling pad,
Sometimes a curly shepherd-lad,
Or long-hair'd page in crimson clad,
 Goes by to tower'd Camelot;
And sometimes thro' the mirror blue
The knights come riding two and two:
She hath no loyal knight and true,
 The Lady of Shalott.

But in her web she still delights
To weave the mirror's magic sights,
For often thro' the silent nights
A funeral, with plumes and lights
 And music, went to Camelot;
Or when the moon was overhead,
Came two young lovers lately wed:
"I am half sick of shadows," said
 The Lady of Shalott.

Part Three

A bow-shot from her bower-eaves,
He rode between the barley-sheaves,
The sun came dazzling thro' the leaves,
And flamed upon the brazen greaves
 Of bold Sir Lancelot.
A red-cross knight for ever kneel'd
To a lady in his shield,

That sparkled on the yellow field,
   Beside remote Shalott.

His broad clear brow in sunlight glow'd;
On burnish'd hooves his war-horse trode;
From underneath his helmet flow'd
His coal-black curls as on he rode,
   As he rode down to Camelot.
From the bank and from the river
He flash'd into the crystal mirror,
"Tirra lirra," by the river
   Sang Sir Lancelot.

She left the web, she left the loom,
She made three paces thro' the room,
She saw the water-lily bloom,
She saw the helmet and the plume,
   She look'd down to Camelot.
Out flew the web and floated wide;
The mirror crack'd from side to side:
"The curse is come upon me," cried
   The Lady of Shalott.

Part Four

In the stormy east-wind straining,
The pale yellow woods were waning,
The broad stream in his banks complaining,
Heavily the low sky raining
   Over tower'd Camelot;
Down she came and found a boat
Beneath a willow left afloat,
And round about the prow she wrote
   The Lady of Shalott.

And down the river's dim expanse—
Like some bold seër in a trance,
Seeing all his own mischance—
With a glassy countenance
   Did she look to Camelot.
And at the closing of the day
She loosed the chain, and down she lay;

The broad stream bore her far away,
   The Lady of Shalott.

Lying, robed in snowy white
That loosely flew to left and right—
The leaves upon her falling light—
Thro' the noises of the night
   She floated down to Camelot;
And as the boat-head wound along
The willowing hills and fields among,
They heard her singing her last song,
   The Lady of Shalott.

Heard a carol, mournful, holy,
Chanted loudly, chanted lowly,
Till her blood was frozen slowly,
And her eyes were darken'd wholly,
   Turn'd to tower'd Camelot.
For ere she reach'd upon the tide
The first house by the water-side,
Singing in her song she died,
   The Lady of Shalott.

Under tower and balcony,
By garden-wall and gallery,
A gleaming shape she floated by,
Dead-pale between the houses high,
   Silent into Camelot.
Out upon the wharfs they came,
Knight and burgher, lord and dame,
And round the prow they read her name,
   The Lady of Shalott.

Who is this? and what is here?
And in the lighted palace near
Died the sound of royal cheer;
And they cross'd themselves for fear,
   All the knights at Camelot:
But Lancelot mused a little space;
He said, "She has a lovely face;
God in His mercy lend her grace,
   The Lady of Shalott."

The Definition of Love
Andrew Marvell

My love is of a birth as rare
As 'tis for object strange and high;
It was begotten by Despair
Upon Impossibility.

Magnanimous Despair alone
Could show me so divine a thing,
Where feeble Hope could ne'er have flown
But vainly flapt its tinsel wing.

And yet I quickly might arrive
Where my extended soul is fixt,
But Fate does iron wedges drive,
And always crowds itself betwixt.

For Fate with jealous eye does see
Two perfect loves, nor lets them close:
Their union would her ruin be,
And her tyrranic pow'r depose.

And therefore her decrees of steel
Us as the distant poles have plac'd,
(Though Love's whole world on us does wheel)
Not by themselves to be embrac'd,

Unless the giddy heaven fall
And earth some new convulsion tear,
And, us to join, the world should all
Be cramp'd into a planisphere.

As lines, so loves oblique may well
Themselves in every angle greet;
But ours, so truly parallel,
Though infinite, can never meet.

Therefore the love which doth us bind,
But Fate so enviously debars,
Is the conjunction of the mind,
And opposition of the stars.

A Woman's Question
Lena Lathrop

Do you know you have asked for the costliest thing
Ever made by the Hand above?
A woman's heart, and a woman's life—
And a woman's wonderful love.

You have written my lesson of duty out;
Manlike, you have questioned me.
Now stand at the bar of my woman's soul
Until I shall question thee.

You require your mutton shall be always hot,
Your socks and your shirt be whole;
I require your heart to be true as God's stars
And as pure as His heaven your soul.

A king for the beautiful realm called Home,
And a man that his Maker, God,
Shall look upon as He did on the first
And say: "It is very good."

I am fair and young, but the rose may fade
From my soft young cheek one day;
Will you love me then 'mid the falling leaves,
As you did 'mong the blossoms of May?

Is your heart an ocean so strong and deep,
I may launch my all on its tide?
A loving woman finds heaven or hell
On the day she is made a bride.

I require all things that are grand and true,
All things that a man should be;
If you give this all, I would stake my life
To be all you demand of me.

If you cannot be this, a laundress and cook
You can hire and little to pay;
But a woman's heart and a woman's life
Are not to be won that way.

LOVE
ROY CROFT

I love you,
Not only for what you are,
But for what I am
When I am with you.

I love you,
Not only for what
You have made of yourself,
But for what
You are making of me.

I love you
For the part of me
That you bring out;
I love you
For putting your hand
Into my heaped-up heart
And passing over
All the foolish, weak things
That you can't help

Dimly seeing there,
And for drawing out
Into the light
All the beautiful belongings
That no one else had looked
Quite far enough to find.

I love you because you
Are helping me to make
Of the lumber of my life
Not a tavern
But a temple;
Out of the works
Of my every day
Not a reproach
But a song.

I love you
Because you have done
More than any creed

Could have done
To make me good,
And more than any fate
Could have done
To make me happy.

You have done it
Without a touch,
Without a word,
Without a sign.
You have done it
By being yourself.
Perhaps that is what
Being a friend means,
After all.

THE PASSIONATE SHEPHERD TO HIS LOVE
CHRISTOPHER MARLOWE

Come live with me and be my love,
And we will all the pleasures prove
That valleys, groves, hills, and fields,
Woods, or steepy mountain yields.

And we will sit upon the rocks,
Seeing the shepherds feed their flocks
By shallow rivers, to whose falls
Melodious birds sing madrigals.

And I will make thee beds of roses
And a thousand fragrant posies,
A cap of flowers and a kirtle
Embroidered all with leaves of myrtle;

A gown made of the finest wool
Which from our pretty lambs we pull;
Fair-linèd slippers for the cold,
With buckles of the purest gold;

A belt of straw and ivy buds,
With coral clasps and amber studs.
And if these pleasures may thee move,
Come live with me and be my love.

The shepherd swains shall dance and sing
For thy delight each May morning.
If these delights thy mind may move,
Then live with me and be my love.

FORGET THEE?
JOHN MOULTRIE

"Forget thee?" If to dream by night and muse on thee by day,
If all the worship deep and wild a poet's heart can pay,
If prayers in absence breathed for thee
    to Heaven's protecting power,
If winged thoughts that flit to thee—a thousand in an hour—
If busy fancy blending thee with all my future lot—
If this thou call'st "forgetting," thou, indeed, shalt be forgot!

"Forget thee?" Bid the forest-birds forget their sweetest tune;
"Forget thee?" Bid the sea forget to swell beneath the moon;
Bid the thirsty flowers forget to drink the eve's refreshing dew;
Thyself forget thine own "dear land,"
    and its "mountains wild and blue."
Forget each old familiar face, each long-remember'd spot—
When these things are forgot by thee, then thou shalt be forgot!

Keep, if thou wilt, thy maiden peace, still calm and fancy-free,
For God forbid thy gladsome heart should grow less glad for me;
Yet, while that heart is still unwon, oh! bid not mine to rove,
But let it nurse its humble faith and uncomplaining love;
If these, preserved for patient years, at last avail me not,
Forget me then; but ne'er believe that thou canst be forgot!

MEETING AT NIGHT
ROBERT BROWNING

The gray sea and the long black land;
And the yellow half-moon large and low;
And the startled little waves that leap
In fiery ringlets from their sleep,
As I gain the cove with pushing prow,
And quench its speed i' the slushy sand.

Then a mile of warm sea-scented beach;
Three fields to cross till a farm appears;
A tap at the pane, the quick sharp scratch
And blue spurt of a lighted match,
And a voice less loud, through its joys and fears,
Than the two hearts beating each to each!

FROM SONNETS FROM THE PORTUGUESE
ELIZABETH BARRETT BROWNING

First time he kissed me, he but only kiss'd
   The fingers of this hand wherewith I write;
   And ever since, it grew more clean and white,
Slow to world-greetings, quick with its "Oh, list,"
When the angels speak. A ring of amethyst
   I could not wear here, plainer to my sight,
   Than that first kiss. The second pass'd in height
The first, and sought the forehead, and half miss'd,
Half falling on the hair. Oh, beyond meed!
   That was the chrism of love, which love's own crown,
With sanctifying sweetness, did precede.
   The third upon my lips was folded down
In perfect, purple state; since when, indeed,
   I have been proud, and said, "My love, my own!"

MISS YOU
DAVID CORY

Miss you, miss you, miss you;
Everything I do
Echoes with the laughter
And the voice of You.
You're on every corner,
Every turn and twist,
Every old familiar spot
Whispers how you're missed.

Miss you, miss you, miss you!
Everywhere I go
There are poignant memories
Dancing in a row.
Silhouette and shadow
Of your form and face,
Substance and reality
Everywhere displace.

Oh, I miss you, miss you!
God! I miss you, Girl!
There's a strange, sad silence
'Mid the busy whirl,
Just as tho' the ordinary
Daily things I do
Wait with me, expectant
For a word from You.

Miss you, miss you, miss you!
Nothing now seems true
Only that 'twas heaven
Just to be with You.

'Twas heaven just
to be
with you

A pair of azure eyes

FROM An Old Sweetheart of Mine
James Whitcomb Riley

As one who cons at evening o'er an album, all alone,
And muses on the faces of the friends that he has known,
So I turn the leaves of Fancy, till, in a shadowy design,
I find the smiling features of an old sweetheart of mine.

The lamplight seems to glimmer with a flicker of surprise,
As I turn it low—to rest me of the dazzle in my eyes,
And light my pipe in silence, save a sigh that seems to yoke
Its fate with my tobacco and to vanish with the smoke.

'Tis a *fragrant* retrospection,—for the loving thoughts that start
Into being are like perfume from the blossom of the heart;
And to dream the old dreams over is a luxury divine—
When my truant fancies wander with that old sweetheart of mine.

Though I hear beneath my study, like a fluttering of wings,
The voices of my children and the mother as she sings—
I feel no twinge of conscience to deny me any theme
When Care has cast her anchor in the harbor of a dream—

In fact, to speak in earnest, I believe it adds a charm
To spice the good a trifle with a little dust of harm,—
For I find an extra flavor in Memory's mellow wine
That makes me drink the deeper to that old sweetheart of mine.

A face of lily beauty, with a form of airy grace,
Floats out of my tobacco as the Genii from the vase;

as tender as the skies . . .

And I thrill beneath the glances of a pair of azure eyes
As glowing as the summer and as tender as the skies.

I can see the pink sunbonnet and the little checkered dress
She wore when first I kissed her and she answered the caress
With the written declaration that, "as surely as the vine
Grew 'round the stump," she loved me—that old sweetheart of mine.

And again I feel the pressure of her slender little hand,
As we used to talk together of the future we had planned,—
When I should be a poet, and with nothing else to do
But write the tender verses that she set the music to . . .

Then we should live together in a cozy little cot
Hid in a nest of roses, with a fairy garden spot,
Where the vines were ever fruited, and the weather ever fine,
And the birds were ever singing for that old sweetheart of mine.

When I should be her lover forever and a day,
And she my faithful sweetheart till the golden hair was gray;
And we should be so happy that when either's lips were dumb
They would not smile in Heaven till the other's kiss had come.

But, ah! my dream is broken by a step upon the stair,
And the door is softly opened, and—my wife is standing there;
Yet with eagerness and rapture all my vision I resign,—
To greet the *living* presence of that old sweetheart of mine.

To My Dear and Loving Husband
ANNE BRADSTREET

If ever two were one, then surely we.
If ever man were lov'd by wife, then thee;
If ever wife was happy in a man,
Compare with me ye women if you can.
I prize thy love more than whole Mines of gold,
Or all the riches that the East doth hold.
My love is such that Rivers cannot quench,
Nor ought but love from thee, give recompense.
Thy love is such I can no way repay,
The heavens reward thee manifold, I pray.
Then while we live, in love lets so persever,
That when we live no more, we may live ever.

Any Wife or Husband
CAROL HAYNES

Let us be guests in one another's house
With deferential "No" and courteous "Yes";
Let us take care to hide our foolish moods
Behind a certain show of cheerfulness.

Let us avoid all sullen silences;
We should find fresh and sprightly things to say;
I must be fearful lest you find me dull,
And you must dread to bore me any way.

Let us knock gently at each other's heart,
Glad of a chance to look within—and yet
Let us remember that to force one's way
Is the unpardoned breach of etiquette.

So shall I be hostess—you, the host—
Until all need for entertainment ends;
We shall be lovers when the last door shuts,
But what is better still—we shall be friends.

You and I
HENRY ALFORD

My hand is lonely for your clasping, dear;
    My ear is tired waiting for your call.
I want your strength to help, your laugh to cheer;
    Heart, soul and senses need you, one and all.
I droop without your full, frank sympathy;
    We ought to be together—you and I;
We want each other so, to comprehend
    The dream, the hope, things planned, or seen, or wrought.
Companion, comforter and guide and friend,
    As much as love asks love, does thought ask thought.
Life is so short, so fast the lone hours fly,
    We ought to be together, you and I.

Her Answer
JOHN BENNETT

Today, dear heart, but just today,
    The sunshine over all,
The roses crimsoning the air
    Along the garden wall!
Then let the dream and dreamer die
    Whate'er shall be, shall be—
Today will still be thine and mine
    To all eternity.

And oh, there is no glory, dear,
    When all the world is done;
There is no splendor lasteth out
    The sinking of the sun;
There is no thing that lasts, not one,
    When we have turned to clay,
But this: you loved me—all the rest
    Fades with the world away.

There is no hand may stop the sand
    From flowing fast away,
But his who turns the whole glass down
    And dreams 'tis all today!

LOVE'S NOT TIME'S FOOL
WILLIAM SHAKESPEARE

Let me not to the marriage of true minds
Admit impediments. Love is not love
Which alters when it alteration finds,
Or bends with the remover to remove:
O, no! it is an ever-fixèd mark
That looks on tempests and is never shaken;
It is the star to every wandering bark,
Whose worth's unknown, although his height be taken.
Love's not Time's fool, though rosy lips and cheeks
Within his bending sickle's compass come;
Love alters not with his brief hours and weeks,
But bears it out even to the edge of doom.
    If this be error and upon me proved,
    I never writ, nor no man ever loved.

FRIENDSHIP
DINAH MARIA MULOCK CRAIK

Oh, the comfort— the inexpressible comfort
    of feeling safe with a person,
Having neither to weigh thoughts,
Nor measure words—but pouring them
All right out—just as they are—
Chaff and grain together—
Certain that a faithful hand will
Take and sift them—
Keep what is worth keeping—
And with the breath of kindness
Blow the rest away.

If ever two were one,

then surely we.

FROM THE LAST RIDE TOGETHER
Robert Browning

I said—Then, dearest, since 'tis so,
Since now at length my fate I know,
Since nothing all my love avails,
Since all my life seemed meant for fails,
    Since this was written and needs must be—
My whole heart rises up to bless
Your name in pride and thankfulness!
Take back the hope you gave—I claim
Only a memory of the same;
And this beside, if you will not blame—
    Your leave for one more last ride with me.

My mistress bent that brow of hers,
Those deep dark eyes where pride demurs
When pity would be softening through,
Fixed me a breathing-while or two
    With life or death in the balance: right!
The blood replenished me again;
My last thought was at least not vain:
I and my mistress, side by side
Shall be together, breathe and ride,
So, one day more am I deified.
    Who knows but the world may end to-night?

Hush! if you saw some western cloud
All billowy-bosomed, over-bowed
By many benedictions—sun's
And moon's and evening-star's at once—
    And so, you, looking and loving best,
Conscious grew, your passion drew
Cloud, sunset, moonrise, star-shine too,
Down on you, near and yet more near,
Till flesh must fade for heaven was here!—
Thus leant she and lingered—joy and fear!
    Thus lay she a moment on my breast.

Then we began to ride. My soul
Smoothed itself out, a long-cramped scroll

Freshening and fluttering in the wind.
Past hopes already lay behind.
    What need to strive with a life awry?
Had I said that, had I done this,
So might I gain, so might I miss.
Might she have loved me? just as well
She might have hated, who can tell!
Where had I been now if the worst befell?
    And here we are riding, she and I.

Fail I alone, in words and deeds?
Why, all men strive and who succeeds?
We rode; it seemed my spirit flew,
Saw other regions, cities new,
    As the world rushed by on either side.
I thought—All labor, yet no less
Bear up beneath their unsuccess.
Look at the end of work, contrast
The petty done, the undone vast,
This present of theirs with the hopeful past!
    I hoped she would love me; here we ride.

What hand and brain went ever paired?
What heart alike conceived and dared?
What act proved all its thought had been?
What will but felt the fleshly screen?
    We ride and I see her bosom heave.
There's many a crown for who can reach.
Ten lines, a statesman's life in each!
The flag stuck on a heap of bones,
A soldier's doing! what atones?
They scratch his name on the Abbey-stones.
    My riding is better, by their leave.

What does it all mean, poet? Well,
Your brains beat into rhythm, you tell
What we felt only; you expressed
You hold things beautiful the best,

And pace them in rhyme so, side by side.
'Tis something, nay 'tis much: but then,
Have you yourself what's best for men?
Are you—poor, sick, old ere your time—
Nearer one whit your own sublime
Than we who never have turned a rhyme?
　　Sing, riding's a joy! For me, I ride.

* * *

Who knows what's fit for us? Had fate
Proposed bliss here should sublimate
My being—had I signed the bond—
Still one must lead some life beyond,
　　Have a bliss to die with, dim-descried.
This foot once planted on the goal,
This glory-garland round my soul,
Could I descry such? Try and test!
I sink back shuddering from the quest.
Earth being so good, would heaven seem best?
　　Now, heaven and she are beyond this ride.

And yet—she has not spoke so long!
What if heaven be that, fair and strong
At life's best, with our eyes upturned
Whither life's flower is first discerned,
　　We, fixed so, ever should so abide?
What if we still ride on, we two
With life for ever old yet new,
Changed not in kind but in degree,
The instant made eternity—
And heaven just prove that I and she
　　Ride, ride together, for ever ride?

*My whole heart rises
up to bless your name.*

Answer to a Child's Question
Samuel Taylor Coleridge

Do you ask what the birds say?
The sparrow, the dove,
The linnet and thrush say,
"I love and I love!"
In the winter they're silent—
The wind is so strong;
What it says, I don't know,
But it sings a loud song.
But green leaves, and blossoms,
And sunny warm weather,
And singing, and loving—
All come back together.
But the lark is so brimful
Of gladness and love,
The green fields below him,
The blue sky above,
That he sings, and he sings;
And for ever sings he—
"I love my Love,
And my Love loves me!"

FROM Rabbi Ben Ezra
Robert Browning

Grow old along with me!
The best is yet to be,
The last of life, for which the first was made:
Our times are in his hand
Who saith: "A whole I planned,
Youth shows but half; trust God, see all, nor be afraid."

Grow old along with me . . .

Moon Compasses
Robert Frost

I stole forth dimly in the dripping pause
Between two downpours to see what there was.
And a masked moon had spread down compass rays
To a cone mountain in the midnight haze,
As if the final estimate were hers;
And as it measured in her calipers,
The mountain stood exalted in its place.
So love will take between the hands a face. . . .

Why So Pale and Wan?
Sir John Suckling

Why so pale and wan, fond lover?
    Prithee, why so pale?
Will, when looking well can't move her,
    Looking ill prevail?
    Prithee, why so pale?

Why so dull and mute, young sinner?
    Prithee, why so mute?
Will, when speaking well can't win her,
    Saying nothing do 't?
    Prithee, why so mute?

Quit, quit for shame! This will not move,
    This cannot take her.
If of herself she will not love,
    Nothing can make her:
    The devil take her!

The best is yet to be.

We Have Lived and Loved Together
CHARLES JEFFERYS

We have lived and loved together
  Through many changing years;
We have shared each other's gladness
  And wept each other's tears;
I have known ne'er a sorrow
  That was long unsoothed by thee;
For thy smiles can make a summer
  Where darkness else would be.

Like the leaves that fall around us
  In autumn's fading hours,
Are the traitor's smiles, that darken
  When the cloud of sorrow lowers;
And though many such we've known, love,
  Too prone, alas, to range,
We both can speak of one love
  Which time can never change.

We have lived and loved together
  Through many changing years;
We have shared each other's gladness
  And wept each other's tears.
And let us hope the future
  As the past has been will be:
I will share with thee my sorrows,
  And thou thy joys with me.

Will You Love Me When I'm Old?
AUTHOR UNKNOWN

I would ask of you, my darling,
  A question soft and low,
That gives me many a heartache
  As the moments come and go.

Your love I know is truthful,
  But the truest love grows cold;
It is this that I would ask you:
  Will you love me when I'm old?

    Life's morn will soon be waning,
      And its evening bells be tolled,
    But my heart shall know no sadness,
      If you'll love me when I'm old.

Down the stream of life together
  We are sailing side by side,
Hoping some bright day to anchor
  Safe beyond the surging tide.
Today our sky is cloudless,
  But the night may clouds unfold;
But, though storms may gather round us,
  Will you love me when I'm old?

When my hair shall shade the snowdrift,
  And mine eyes shall dimmer grow,
I would lean upon some loved one,
  Through the valley as I go.
I would claim of you a promise,
  Worth to me a world of gold;
It is only this, my darling,
  That you'll love me when I'm old.

ANNABEL LEE
EDGAR ALLAN POE

It was many and many a year ago,
    In a kingdom by the sea,
That a maiden there lived, whom you may know
    By the name of Annabel Lee;
And this maiden she lived with no other thought
    Than to love, and be loved by me.

I was a child and she was a child,
    In this kingdom by the sea;
But we loved with a love that was more than love,
    I and my Annabel Lee,—
With a love that the wingèd seraphs of heaven
    Coveted her and me.

The angels, not so happy in heaven,
    Went envying her and me.
Yes! that was the reason (as all men know)
    In this kingdom by the sea,
That the wind came out of the cloud by night,
    Chilling and killing my Annabel Lee.

But our love it was stronger by far than the love
    Of those who were older than we,
    Of many far wiser than we;
And neither the angels in heaven above,
    Nor the demons down under the sea,
Can ever dissever my soul from the soul
    Of the beautiful Annabel Lee.

For the moon never beams without bringing me dreams
    Of the beautiful Annabel Lee,
And the stars never rise but I feel the bright eyes
    Of the beautiful Annabel Lee.
And so, all the night-tide I lie down by the side
Of my darling, my darling, my life, and my bride,
    In her sepulchre there by the sea,
    In her tomb by the sounding sea.

IN A ROSE GARDEN
JOHN BENNETT

A hundred years from now, dear heart,
    We shall not care at all,
It will not matter then a whit,
    The honey or the gall.
The summer days that we have known
Will all forgotten be and flown;
The garden will be overgrown
    Where now the roses fall.

A hundred years from now, dear heart,
    We shall not mind the pain;
The throbbing crimson tide of life
    Will not have left a stain.
The song we sing together, dear,
The dream we dream together here,
Will mean no more than means a tear
    Amid a summer rain.

A hundred years from now, dear heart,
    The grief will all be o'er;
The sea of care will surge in vain
    Upon a careless shore.
These glasses we turn down today
Here at the parting of the way—
We shall be wineless then as they,
    And shall not mind it more.

A hundred years from now, dear heart,
    We'll neither know nor care
What came of all life's bitterness,
    Or followed love's despair.
Then fill the glasses up again,
And kiss me through the rose-leaf rain;
We'll build one castle more in Spain,
    And dream one more dream there.

Poems Tell a

LOVE'S SECRET
WILLIAM BLAKE

Never seek to tell thy love,
   Love that never told can be;

For the gentle wind doth move
   Silently, invisibly.

That Story

I told my love, I told my love,
    I told her all my heart,
Trembling, cold, in ghastly fears
    Ah! she did depart!

Soon after she was gone from me,
    A traveller came by,
Silently, invisibly:
    He took her with a sigh.

THE ONE-HOSS SHAY
(THE DEACON'S MASTERPIECE)
OLIVER WENDELL HOLMES

Have you heard of the wonderful one-hoss shay,
That was built in such a logical way
It ran a hundred years to a day,
And then, of a sudden, it—ah, but stay,
I'll tell you what happened without delay,
Scaring the parson into fits,
Frightening people out of their wits,—
Have you ever heard of that, I say?

Seventeen hundred and fifty-five.
Georgius Secundus was then alive,—
Snuffy old drone from the German hive.
That was the year when Lisbon-town
Saw the earth open and gulp her down,
And Braddock's army was done so brown,
Left without a scalp to its crown.
It was on the terrible Earthquake-day
That the Deacon finished the one-hoss shay.

Now in building of chaises, I tell you what,
There is always *somewhere* a weaker spot,—
In hub, tire, felloe, in spring or thill,
In panel, or crossbar, or floor, or sill,
In screw, bolt, thoroughbrace,—lurking still,
Find it somewhere you must and will,—
Above or below, or within or without,—
And that's the reason, beyond a doubt,
A chaise *breaks down,* but doesn't *wear out.*

But the Deacon swore (as Deacons do),
With an "I dew vum," or an "I tell yeou,"
He would build one shay to beat the taown
'N' the keounty 'n' all the kentry raoun';
It should be so built that it *couldn'* break daown:
—"Fur," said the Deacon, "t's mighty plain
Thut the weakes' place mus' stan' the strain;
'N' the way t' fix it, uz I maintain,
   Is only jest
T' make that place uz strong uz the rest."

So the Deacon inquired of the village folk
Where he could find the strongest oak,
That couldn't be split nor bent nor broke,—
That was for spokes and floor and sills;
He sent for lancewood to make the thills;
The crossbars were ash, from the straightest trees,
The panels of white-wood, that cuts like cheese,
But lasts like iron for things like these;
The hubs of logs from the "Settler's ellum,"—
Last of its timber,—they couldn't sell 'em,
Never an axe had seen their chips,
And the wedges flew from between their lips,
Their blunt ends frizzled like celery tips;
Step and prop-iron, bolt and screw,
Spring, tire, axle, and linchpin too,
Steel of the finest, bright and blue;
Thoroughbrace bison-skin, thick and wide;
Boot, top, dasher, from tough old hide
Found in the pit when the tanner died.
That was the way he "put her through."—
"There!" said the Deacon, "naow she'll dew!"

Do! I tell you, I rather guess
She was a wonder, and nothing less!
Colts grew horses, beards turned gray,
Deacon and Deaconess dropped away,
Children and grandchildren—where were they?
But there stood the stout old one-hoss shay
As fresh as on Lisbon-earthquake-day!

EIGHTEEN HUNDRED;—it came and found
The Deacon's masterpiece strong and sound.
Eighteen hundred increased by ten;—
"Hahnsum kerridge" they called it then.
Eighteen hundred and twenty came;—
Running as usual; much the same.
Thirty and forty at last arrive,
And then come fifty, and FIFTY-FIVE.

FIRST OF NOVEMBER—the-Earthquake-day,—
There are traces of age in the one-hoss-shay,
A general flavor of mild decay,

But nothing local, as one may say.
There couldn't be,—for the Deacon's art
Had made it so like in every part
That there wasn't a chance for one to start.
For the wheels were just as strong as the thills,
And the floor was just as strong as the sills,
And the panels just as strong as the floor,
And the whipple-tree neither less nor more,
And the back-cross bar as strong as the fore,
And spring and axle and hub *encore.*
And yet, as a *whole,* it is past a doubt
In another hour it will be *worn out!*

First of November, 'Fifty-five!
This morning the parson takes a drive.
Now, small boys, get out of the way!
Here comes the wonderful one-hoss shay,
Drawn by a rat-tailed, ewe-necked bay.
"Huddup!" said the parson. Off went they.
The parson was working his Sunday text,—
Had got to *fifthly,* and stopped perplexed
At what the—Moses—was coming next.
All at once the horse stood still,
Close by the meet'n'-house on the hill.
—First a shiver, and then a thrill,
Then something decidedly like a spill,—
And the parson was sitting up on a rock,
At half-past nine by the meet'n'-house clock,—
Just the hour of the Earthquake shock!
—What do you think the parson found,
When he got up and stared around?
The poor old chaise in a heap or mound,
As if it had been to the mill and ground!
You see, of course, if you're not a dunce,
How it went to pieces all at once,—
All at once, and nothing first,—
Just as bubbles do when they burst.

End of the wonderful one-hoss shay,
Logic is logic. That's all I say.

The strongest oak . . .

A ribbon of moonlight

THE HIGHWAYMAN
ALFRED NOYES

The wind was a torrent of darkness among the gusty trees,
The moon was a ghostly galleon tossed upon cloudy seas,
The road was a ribbon of moonlight over the purple moor,
And the highwayman came riding—
    Riding—riding—
The highwayman came riding, up to the old inn-door.

He'd a French cock-hat on his forehead, a bunch of lace at his chin,
A coat of the claret velvet, and breeches of brown doe-skin;
They fitted with never a wrinkle: his boots were up to the thigh!
And he rode with a jeweled twinkle,
    His pistol butts a-twinkle,
His rapier hilt a-twinkle, under the jeweled sky.

Over the cobbles he clattered and clashed in the dark inn-yard,
And he tapped with his whip on the shutters, but all was locked and barred;
He whistled a tune to the window, and who should be waiting there
But the landlord's black-eyed daughter,
    Bess, the landlord's daughter,
Plaiting a dark red love-knot into her long black hair.

And dark in the dark old inn-yard, a stable-wicket creaked
Where Tim the ostler listened; his face was white and peaked;
His eyes were hollows of madness, his hair like mouldy clay,
But he loved the landlord's daughter,
    The landlord's red-lipped daughter,
Dumb as a dog he listened, and he heard the robber say—

over the purple moor.

"One kiss, my bonny sweetheart, I'm after a prize to-night,
But I shall be back with the yellow gold before the morning light;
Yet, if they press me sharply, and harry me through the day,
Then look for me by moonlight,
     Watch for me by moonlight,
I'll come to thee by moonlight, though hell should bar the way."

He rose upright in his stirrups; he scarce could reach her hand,
But she loosened her hair i' the casement! His face burnt like a brand
As the black cascade of perfume came tumbling over his breast;
And he kissed its waves in the moonlight,
     (Oh, sweet black waves in the moonlight!)
Then he tugged at his reins in the moonlight, and galloped away to the West.

He did not come in the dawning; he did not come at noon;
And out o' the tawny sunset, before the rise o' the moon,
When the road was a gipsy's ribbon, looping the purple moor,
A red-coat troop came marching—
     Marching—marching—
King George's men came marching, up to the old inn-door.

They said no word to the landlord, they drank his ale instead,
But they gagged his daughter and bound her to the foot of her narrow bed;
Two of them knelt at her casement, with muskets at their side!
There was death at every window;
     And hell at one dark window;
For Bess could see, through her casement, the road that he would ride.

They had tied her up to attention, with many a sniggering jest:
They had bound a musket beside her, with the barrel beneath her breast!
"Now keep good watch!" and they kissed her.
    She heard the dead man say—
Look for me by moonlight;
   Watch for me by moonlight;
I'll come to thee by moonlight, though hell should bar the way!

She twisted her hands behind her; but all the knots held good!
She writhed her hands till her fingers were wet with sweat or blood!
They stretched and strained in the darkness, and the hours crawled by like years,
Till, now, on the stroke of midnight,
    Cold, on the stroke of midnight,
The tip of one finger touched it! The trigger at least was hers!

The tip of one finger touched it; she strove no more for the rest!
Up, she stood up to attention, with the barrel beneath her breast,
She would not risk their hearing; she would not strive again;
For the road lay bare in the moonlight;
And the blood of her veins in the moonlight throbbed to her love's refrain.

Tlot-tlot; tlot-tlot! Had they heard it? The horse-hoofs ringing clear;
Tlot-tlot, tlot-tlot, in the distance? Were they deaf that they did not hear?
Down the ribbon of moonlight, over the brow of the hill,
The highwayman came riding,
    Riding, riding!
The red-coats looked to their priming! She stood up, straight and still!

Tlot-tlot, in the frosty silence! *Tlot-tlot,* in the echoing night!
Nearer he came and nearer! Her face was like a light!
Her eyes grew wide for a moment; she drew one last deep breath,

by moonlight . . .

Then her finger moved in the moonlight,
   Her musket shattered the moonlight,
Shattered her breast in the moonlight and warned him—with her death.

He turned; he spurred to the West; he did not know who stood
Bowed, with her head o'er the musket, drenched with her own red blood!
Not till the dawn he heard it, his face grew gray to hear
How Bess, the landlord's daughter,
   The landlord's black-eyed daughter,
Had watched for her love in the moonlight, and died in the darkness there.

Back he spurred like a madman, shrieking a curse to the sky,
With the white road smoking behind him and his rapier brandished high!
Blood-red were his spurs i' the golden noon; wine-red was his velvet coat,
When they shot him down in the highway,
   Down like a dog in the highway,
And he lay in his blood on the highway, with the bunch of lace at his throat.

And still of a winter's night, they say, when the wind is in the trees,
When the moon is a ghostly galleon tossed upon cloudy seas,
When the road is a ribbon of moonlight over the purple moor,
A highwayman comes riding—
   Riding—riding—
A highwayman comes riding, up to the old inn-door.

Over the cobbles he clatters and clangs in the dark inn-yard;
He taps with his whip on the shutters, but all is locked and barred;
He whistles a tune at the window, and who should be waiting there
But the landlord's black-eyed daughter,
   Bess, the landlord's daughter,
Plaiting a dark red love-knot into her long black hair.

CASEY AT THE BAT
ERNEST LAWRENCE THAYER

It looked extremely rocky for the Mudville nine that day;
The score stood two to four, with but one inning left to play.
So, when Cooney died at second, and Burrows did the same,
A pallor wreathed the features of the patrons of the game.

A straggling few got up to go, leaving there the rest,
With that hope which springs eternal within the human breast.
For they thought: "If only Casey could get a whack at that,"
They'd put even money now, with Casey at the bat.

But Flynn preceded Casey, and likewise so did Blake,
And the former was a pudd'n, and the latter was a fake.
So on that stricken multitude a deathlike silence sat;
For there seemed but little chance of Casey's getting to the bat.

But Flynn let drive a "single," to the wonderment of all.
And the much-despisèd Blakey "tore the cover off the ball."
And when the dust had lifted, and they saw what had occurred,
There was Blakey safe at second, and Flynn a-huggin' third.

Then from the gladdened multitude went up a joyous yell—
It rumbled in the mountaintops, it rattled in the dell;
It struck upon the hillside and rebounded on the flat;
For Casey, mighty Casey, was advancing to the bat.

There was ease in Casey's manner as he stepped into his place,
There was pride in Casey's bearing and a smile on Casey's face;
And when responding to the cheers he lightly doffed his hat,
No stranger in the crowd could doubt 'twas Casey at the bat.

Ten thousand eyes were on him as he rubbed his hands with dirt,
Five thousand tongues applauded when he wiped them on his shirt;

Casey, mighty Casey, was

Then when the writhing pitcher ground the ball into his hip,
Defiance glanced in Casey's eye, a sneer curled Casey's lip.

And now the leather-covered sphere came hurtling through the air,
And Casey stood a-watching it in haughty grandeur there.
Close by the sturdy batsman the ball unheeded sped;
"That ain't my style," said Casey. "Strike one," the umpire said.

From the benches, black with people, there went up a muffled roar,
Like the beating of the storm waves on the stern and distant shore.
"Kill him! kill the umpire!" shouted someone on the stand;
And it's likely they'd have killed him had not Casey raised his hand.

With a smile of Christian charity great Casey's visage shone;
He stilled the rising tumult, he made the game go on;
He signaled to the pitcher, and once more the spheroid flew;
But Casey still ignored it, and the umpire said, "Strike two."

"Fraud!" cried the maddened thousands, and the echo answered "Fraud!"
But one scornful look from Casey and the audience was awed;
They saw his face grow stern and cold, they saw his muscles strain,
And they knew that Casey wouldn't let the ball go by again.

The sneer is gone from Casey's lips, his teeth are clenched in hate,
He pounds with cruel vengeance his bat upon the plate;
And now the pitcher holds the ball, and now he lets it go,
And now the air is shattered by the force of Casey's blow.

Oh, somewhere in this favored land the sun is shining bright,
The band is playing somewhere, and somewhere hearts are light;
And somewhere men are laughing, and somewhere children shout,
But there is no joy in Mudville—Mighty Casey has struck out.

advancing to the bat . . .

'Tis the wind,

THE RAVEN
EDGAR ALLAN POE

Once upon a midnight dreary, while I pondered, weak and weary,
Over many a quaint and curious volume of forgotten lore—
While I nodded, nearly napping, suddenly there came a tapping,
As of some one gently rapping, rapping at my chamber door.
"'Tis some visitor," I muttered, "tapping at my chamber door:
   Only this, and nothing more."

Ah, distinctly I remember, it was in the bleak December,
And each separate dying ember wrought its ghost upon the floor.
Eagerly I wished the morrow; vainly I had sought to borrow
From my books surcease of sorrow—sorrow for the lost Lenore—
For the rare and radiant maiden whom the angels named Lenore—
   Nameless here for evermore.

And the silken, sad, uncertain rustling of each purple curtain,
Thrilled me—filled me with fantastic terrors never felt before;
So that now, to still the beating of my heart, I stood repeating,
"'Tis some visitor entreating entrance at my chamber door—
Some late visitor entreating entrance at my chamber door:
   This it is, and nothing more."

Presently my soul grew stronger: hesitating then no longer,
"Sir," said I, "or Madam, truly your forgiveness I implore;
But the fact is, I was napping, and so gently you came rapping,
And so faintly you came tapping, tapping at my chamber door,
That I scarce was sure I heard you"—here I opened wide the door;—
   Darkness there, and nothing more!

Deep into that darkness peering, long I stood there, wondering, fearing,
Doubting, dreaming dreams no mortal ever dared to dream before;

and nothing more . . .

But the silence was unbroken, and the darkness gave no token,
And the only word there spoken was the whispered word, "Lenore!"
This I whispered, and an echo murmured back the word "Lenore!"
    Merely this, and nothing more.

Back into the chamber turning, all my soul within me burning,
Soon again I heard a tapping, somewhat louder than before.
"Surely," said I, "surely that is something at my window-lattice;
Let me see then what thereat is, and this mystery explore—
Let my heart be still a moment, and this mystery explore;—
    'Tis the wind, and nothing more!"

Open here I flung the shutter, when, with many a flirt and flutter,
In there stepped a stately Raven of the saintly days of yore.
Not the least obeisance made he; not an instant stopped or stayed he;
But, with mien of lord or lady, perched above my chamber door—
Perched upon a bust of Pallas, just above my chamber door—
    Perched, and sat, and nothing more.

Then this ebony bird beguiling my sad fancy into smiling,
By the grave and stern decorum of the countenance it wore,
"Though thy crest be shorn and shaven, thou," I said, "art sure no craven,
Ghastly, grim, and ancient Raven, wandering from the nightly shore!
Tell me what thy lordly name is on the night's Plutonian shore!"
    Quoth the Raven, "Nevermore!"

Much I marveled this ungainly fowl to hear discourse so plainly,
Though its answer little meaning—little relevancy bore:
For we cannot help agreeing that no living human being
Ever yet was blessed with seeing bird above his chamber door—
Bird or beast upon the sculptured bust above his chamber door.
    With such name as "Nevermore!"

Quoth the raven,

But the Raven, sitting lonely on the placid bust, spoke only
That one word, as if his soul in that one word he did outpour.
Nothing further then he uttered—not a feather then he fluttered—
Till I scarcely more than muttered, "Other friends have flown before—
On the morrow *he* will leave me, as my hopes have flown before."
    Then the bird said, "Nevermore!"

Startled at the stillness broken by reply so aptly spoken,
"Doubtless," said I, "what it utters is its only stock and store,
Caught from some unhappy master, whom unmerciful Disaster
Followed fast and followed faster, till his songs one burden bore—
Till the dirges of his Hope one melancholy burden bore
    Of 'Never—nevermore.'"

But the Raven still beguiling all my sad soul into smiling,
Straight I wheeled a cushioned seat in front of bird, and bust, and door;
Then, upon the velvet sinking, I betook myself to linking
Fancy unto fancy, thinking what this ominous bird of yore—
What this grim, ungainly, ghastly, gaunt, and ominous bird of yore—
    Meant in croaking "Nevermore!"

This I sat engaged in guessing, but no syllable expressing
To the fowl whose fiery eyes now burned into my bosom's core;
This and more I sat divining, with my head at ease reclining
On the cushion's velvet lining that the lamplight gloated o'er,
But whose velvet violet lining, with the lamplight gloating o'er,
    She shall press, ah! nevermore!

Then methought the air grew denser, perfumed from an unseen censer,
Swung by seraphim, whose footfalls tinkled on the tufted floor.
"Wretch," I cried, "thy God hath lent thee—by these angels he hath sent thee
Respite—respite and nepenthe from the memories of Lenore!

"Nevermore!"

Quaff, Oh, quaff this kind nepenthe, and forget this lost Lenore!"
  Quoth the raven, "Nevermore!"

"Prophet!" said I, "thing of evil!—prophet still, if bird or devil!
Whether tempter sent, or whether tempest tossed thee here ashore,
Desolate yet all undaunted, on this desert land enchanted—
On this home by horrors haunted—tell me truly, I implore—
Is there—*is there* balm in Gilead?—tell me—tell me, I implore!"
  Quoth the raven, "Nevermore!"

"Prophet!" said I, "thing of evil!—prophet still, if bird or devil!
By that heaven that bends above us—by that God we both adore,
Tell this soul with sorrow laden if, within the distant Aidenn,
It shall clasp a sainted maiden, whom the angels name Lenore—
Clasp a fair and radiant maiden, whom the angels named Lenore!"
  Quoth the raven, "Nevermore!"

"Be that word our sign of parting, bird or fiend!" I shrieked, upstarting—
"Get thee back into the tempest and the night's Plutonian shore!
Leave no black plume as a token of that lie thy soul hath spoken!
Leave my loneliness unbroken!—quit the bust above my door!
Take thy beak from out my heart, and take thy form from off my door!"
  Quoth the raven, "Nevermore!"

And the raven, never flitting, still is sitting, still is sitting
On the pallid bust of Pallas, just above my chamber door;
And his eyes have all the seeming of a demon that is dreaming,
And the lamplight o'er him streaming throws his shadow on the floor;
And my soul from out that shadow that lies floating on the floor
  Shall be lifted—*nevermore!*

THE RAGGEDY MAN
JAMES WHITCOMB RILEY

O The Raggedy Man! He works fer Pa;
An' he's the goodest man ever you saw!
He comes to our house every day,
An' waters the horses, an' feeds 'em hay;
An' he opens the shed—an' we all ist laugh
When he drives out our little old wobble-ly calf;
An' nen—ef our hired girl says he can–
He milks the cow fer 'Lizabuth Ann,—
    Ain't he a' awful good Raggedy Man?
    Raggedy! Raggedy! Raggedy Man!

W'y, The Raggedy Man—he ist so good
He splits the kindlin' an' chops the wood;
An' nen he spades in our garden, too,
An' does most things 'at *boys* can't do!—
He clumbed clean up in our big tree
An' shooked a' apple down fer me—
An' nother'n, too, fer 'Lizabuth Ann—
An' nother'n, too, fer The Raggedy Man,—
    Ain't he a' awful kind Raggedy Man!
    Raggedy! Raggedy! Raggedy Man!

The Raggedy Man—one time when he
Wuz makin' a little bow-'n'-orry fer me,
Says "When *you're* big like your Pa is,
Air *you* go' to keep a fine store like his—
An' be a rich merchunt—an' wear fine clothes?—
Er what *air* you go' to be, goodness knows!"
An' nen he laughed at 'Lizabuth Ann,
An' I says "M go' to be a Raggedy Man!—
    I'm ist go' to be a nice Raggedy Man!"
    Raggedy! Raggedy! Raggedy Man!

THE VILLAGE BLACKSMITH

Henry Wadsworth Longfellow

Under a spreading chestnut-tree
The village smithy stands;
The smith, a mighty man is he,
With large and sinewy hands;
And the muscles of his brawny arms
Are strong as iron bands.

His hair is crisp, and black, and long,
His face is like the tan;
His brow is wet with honest sweat,
He earns whate'er he can,
And looks the whole world in the face,
For he owes not any man.

Week in, week out, from morn till night,
You can hear his bellows blow;
You can hear him swing his heavy sledge,
With measured beat and slow,
Like a sexton ringing the village bell,
When the evening sun is low.

And children coming home from school
Look in at the open door;
They love to see the flaming forge,
And hear the bellows roar,
And catch the burning sparks that fly
Like chaff from a threshing-floor.

He goes on Sunday to the church,
And sits among his boys;
He hears the parson pray and preach,
He hears his daughter's voice
Singing in the village choir,
And it makes his heart rejoice.

It sounds to him like her mother's voice,
Singing in Paradise!
He needs must think of her once more,
How in the grave she lies;
And with his hard, rough hand he wipes
A tear out of his eyes.

Toiling—rejoicing—sorrowing,
Onward through life he goes;
Each morning sees some task begin,
Each evening sees it close;
Something attempted, something done,
Has earned a night's repose.

Thanks, thanks to thee, my worthy friend,
For the lesson thou hast taught!
Thus at the flaming forge of life
Our fortunes must be wrought;
Thus on its sounding anvil shaped
Each burning deed and thought!

The Landing of the Pilgrim Fathers in New England

Felicia D. Hemans

The breaking waves dashed high
　　On a stern and rock-bound coast,
And the woods against a stormy sky
　　Their giant branches tossed;

And the heavy night hung dark
　　The hills and waters o'er,
When a band of exiles moored their bark
　　On the wild New England shore.

Not as the conqueror comes,
　　They, the true-hearted, came;
Not with the roll of the stirring drums,
　　And the trumpet that sings of fame:

Amidst the storm they sang,
　　And the stars heard, and the sea;
And the sounding aisles of the dim woods rang
　　To the anthem of the free.

There were men with hoary hair
　　Amidst that pilgrim-band:
Why had they come to wither there,
　　Away from their childhood's land?

There was woman's fearless eye,
　　Lit by her deep love's truth;
There was manhood's brow serenely high,
　　And the fiery heart of youth.

What sought they thus afar?
　　Bright jewels of the mine?
The wealth of seas, the spoils of war?—
　　They sought a faith's pure shrine!

Ay, call it holy ground,
　　The soil where first they trod;
They have left unstained what there they found,—
　　Freedom to worship God.

CASEY JONES
AUTHOR UNKNOWN

Come all you rounders for I want you to hear
The story told of a brave engineer;
Casey Jones was the rounder's name
On a heavy six-wheeler he rode to fame.

Caller called Jones about half past four,
Jones kissed his wife at the station door,
Climbed into the cab with the orders in his hand,
Says, "This is my trip to the promised land."

Through South Memphis yards on the fly,
He heard the fireman say, "You've got a white eye."
All the switchmen knew by the engine's moans,
That the hogger at the throttle was Casey Jones.

Fireman says, "Casey, you're runnin' too fast,
You run the block signal the last station you passed."
Jones says, "Yes, I think we can make it, though,
For she steams much better than ever I know."

Jones says, "Fireman, don't you fret,
Keep knockin' at the firedoor, don't give up yet;
I'm goin' to run her till she leaves the rail
Or make it on time with the southbound mail."

Around the curve and a-down the dump,
Two locomotives were a-bound to bump,
Fireman hollered, "Jones, it's just ahead,
We might jump and make it but we'll all be dead."

'Twas around this curve he saw the passenger train,
Something happened in Casey's brain;
Fireman jumped off, but Jones stayed on,
He's a good engineer but he's dead and gone.

Poor Casey Jones was always all right,
He stuck to his post both day and night;
They loved to hear the whistle of old Number Three
As he came into Memphis on the old K.C.

The fiery heart of youth . . . .

My Last Duchess
Robert Browning

That's my last Duchess painted on the wall,
Looking as if she were alive. I call
That piece a wonder, now: Frà Pandolf's hands
Worked busily a day, and there she stands.
Will 't please you sit and look at her? I said
"Frà Pandolf" by design, for never read
Strangers like you that pictured countenance,
The depth and passion of its earnest glance,
But to myself they turned (since none puts by
The curtain I have drawn for you, but I)
And seemed as they would ask me, if they durst
How such a glance came there; so, not the first
Are you to turn and ask thus. Sir, 't was not
Her husband's presence only, called that spot
Of joy into the Duchess' cheek: perhaps
Frà Pandolf chanced to say, "Her mantle laps
Over my lady's wrist too much," or "Paint
Must never hope to reproduce the faint
Half-flush that dies along her throat:" such stuff
Was courtesy, she thought, and cause enough
For calling up that spot of joy. She had
A heart—how shall I say?—too soon made glad.
Too easily impressed: she liked whate'er
She looked on, and her looks went everywhere.
Sir, 't was all one! My favor at her breast,
The dropping of the daylight in the West,
The bough of cherries some officious fool
Broke in the orchard for her, the white mule
She rode with round the terrace—all and each
Would draw from her alike the approving speech,
Or blush, at least. She thanked men—good! but thanked
Somehow—I know not how—as if she ranked
My gift of a nine-hundred-years-old name
With anybody's gift. Who'd stoop to blame
This sort of trifling? Even had you skill
In speech—(which I have not)—to make your will
Quite clear to such an one, and say, "Just this

Her house was out of doors.

Or that in you disgusts me; here you miss,
Or there exceed the mark"—and if she let
Herself be lessoned so, nor plainly set
Her wits to yours, forsooth, and made excuse,
Even then would be some stooping; and I choose
Never to stoop. Oh sir, she smiled, no doubt,
Whenever I passed her; but who passed without
Much the same smile? This grew; I gave commands;
Then all smiles stopped together. There she stands
As if alive. Will 't please you rise? We'll meet
The company below, then. I repeat,
The Count your master's known munificence
Is ample warrant that no just pretence
Of mine for dowry will be disallowed;
Though his fair daughter's self, as I avowed
At starting, is my object. Nay, we'll go
Together down, sir. Notice Neptune, though,
Taming a sea-horse, thought a rarity,
Which Claus of Innsbruck cast in bronze for me!

OLD MEG
JOHN KEATS

Old Meg she was a Gipsey,
    And liv'd upon the Moors;
Her bed it was the brown heath turf,
    And her house was out of doors.

Her apples were swart blackberries,
    Her currants, pods o' broom;
Her wine was dew of the wild white rose,
    Her book a churchyard tomb.

Her Brothers were the craggy hills,
    Her Sisters larchen trees;
Alone with her great family
    She liv'd as she did please.

No breakfast had she many a morn,
    No dinner many a noon,
And, 'stead of supper, she would stare
    Full hard against the moon.

But every morn, of woodbine fresh
    She made her garlanding,
And, every night, the dark glen Yew
    She wove, and she would sing.

And with her fingers, old and brown,
    She plaited Mats o' Rushes,
And gave them to the cottagers
    She met among the Bushes.

Old Meg was brave as Margaret Queen
    And tall as Amazon;
An old red blanket cloak she wore,
    A chip hat had she on.
God rest her aged bones somewhere!
    She died full long agone!

The elephant

THE BLIND MEN AND THE ELEPHANT
JOHN GODFREY SAXE

It was six men of Indostan
    To learning much inclined,
Who went to see the elephant
    (Though all of them were blind),
That each by observation
    Might satisfy his mind.

The First approached the elephant,
    And, happening to fall
Against his broad and sturdy side,
    At once began to bawl:
"God bless me! but the elephant
    Is nothing but a wall!"

The Second, feeling of the tusk,
    Cried: "Ho! what have we here
So very round and smooth and sharp?
    To me 'tis mighty clear
This wonder of an elephant
    Is very like a spear!"

The Third approached the animal,
    And, happening to take
The squirming trunk within his hands,
    Thus boldly up and spake:
"I see," quoth he, "the elephant
    Is very like a snake!"

The Fourth reached out his eager hand,
    And felt about the knee:

is very like a tree

"What most this wondrous beast is like
    Is mighty plain," quoth he;
"'Tis clear enough the elephant
    Is very like a tree."

The Fifth, who chanced to touch the ear,
    Said: "E'en the blindest man
Can tell what this resembles most;
    Deny the fact who can,
This marvel of an elephant
    Is very like a fan!"

The Sixth no sooner had begun
    About the beast to grope,
Than, seizing on the swinging tail
    That fell within his scope,

"I see," quoth he, "the elephant
    Is very like a rope!"

And so these men of Indostan
    Disputed loud and long,
Each in his own opinion
    Exceeding stiff and strong,
Though each was partly in the right.
    And all were in the wrong!

So, oft in theologic wars
    The disputants, I ween,
Rail on in utter ignorance
    Of what each other mean,
And prate about an elephant
    Not one of them has seen!

Poems to

HIGH ADVENTURE
A. W. SPALDING

As I have seen a child,
Round-eyed and innocent,
Leaving his treasured playthings piled

Where new adventure overtook,
Climb up a little staired ascent,
Holding in fear his parent's hand,
And, trepidant with fresh alarms
Yet gathering courage from each trustful look,
With utter confidence in a last command,

Inspire

Fling himself laughing into his father's arms—
So I, another child,
Holding my Father's hand,
Now from my busy arts beguiled
By what He promises beyond,
Forgetting all that I have planned,

And pressing on with faith's sure sight
O'er rock and ridge, through mists and storms,
With confidence that swallows up despond,
From the last crag of life's most glorious height
Cast me exultant into my Father's arms.

The Common Road

Silas H. Perkins

I want to travel the common road
With the great crowd surging by,
Where there's a many a laugh and many a load,
And many a smile and sigh.
I want to be on the common way
With its endless tramping feet,
In the summer bright and winter gray,
In the noonday sun and heat.
In the cool of evening with shadows nigh,
At dawn, when the sun breaks clear,
I want the great crowd passing by,
To ken what they see and hear.
I want to be one of the common herd,
Not live in a sheltered way,
Want to be thrilled, want to be stirred
By the great crowd day by day;

To glimpse the restful valleys deep,
To toil up the rugged hill,
To see the brooks which shyly creep,
To have the torrents thrill.
I want to laugh with the common man
Wherever he chance to be,
I want to aid him when I can
Whenever there's need of me.
I want to lend a helping hand
Over the rough and steep
To a child too young to understand—
To comfort those who weep.
I want to live and work and plan
With the great crowd surging by,
To mingle with the common man,
No better or worse than I.

Hold Fast Your Dreams

Louise Driscoll

Hold fast your dreams!
Within your heart
Keep one still, secret spot
Where dreams may go,
And, sheltered so,
May thrive and grow
Where doubt and fear are not.
O keep a place apart,
Within your heart,
For little dreams to go!

Think still of lovely things that are not true.
Let wish and magic work at will in you.
Be sometimes blind to sorrow. Make believe!
Forget the calm that lies
In disillusioned eyes.
Though we all know that we must die,

Yet you and I
May walk like gods and be
Even now at home in immortality.

We see so many ugly things—
Deceits and wrongs and quarrelings;
We know, alas! we know
How quickly fade
The color in the west,
The bloom upon the flower,
The bloom upon the breast
And youth's blind hour.
Yet keep within your heart
A place apart
Where little dreams may go,
May thrive and grow.
Hold fast—hold fast your dreams!

THE PATH THAT LEADS TO NOWHERE
CORINNE ROOSEVELT ROBINSON

There's a path that leads to Nowhere
   In a meadow that I know,
Where an inland river rises
   And the stream is still and slow;
There it wanders under willows
   And beneath the silver green
Of the birches' silent shadows
   Where the early violets lean.

Other pathways lead to Somewhere,
   But the one I love so well
Had no end and no beginning—
   Just the beauty of the dell,
Just the windflowers and the lilies
   Yellow striped as adder's tongue,
Seem to satisfy my pathway
   As it winds their sweets among.

There I go to meet the Springtime,
   When the meadow is aglow,
Marigolds amid the marshes,
   And the stream is still and slow;
There I find my fair oasis,
   And with carefree feet I tread
For the pathway leads to Nowhere,
   And the blue is overhead.

All the ways that lead to Somewhere
   Echo with the hurrying feet
Of the Struggling and the Striving,
   But the way I find so sweet
Bids me dream and bids me linger—
   Joy and Beauty are its goal;
On the path that leads to Nowhere
   I have sometimes found my soul.

One still, secret spot
where dreams may go . . .

THE LAND OF BEGINNING AGAIN
LOUISA FLETCHER

I wish that there were some wonderful place
    Called the Land of Beginning Again,
Where all our mistakes and all our heartaches
    And all of our poor selfish grief
Could be dropped like a shabby old coat at the door,
    And never be put on again.

I wish we could come on it all unaware,
    Like the hunter who finds a lost trail;
And I wish that the one whom our blindness had done
    The greatest injustice of all
Could be at the gates like an old friend that waits
    For the comrade he's gladdest to hail.

We would find all the things we intended to do
    But forgot, and remembered too late,
Little praises unspoken, little promises broken,
    And all of the thousand and one
Little duties neglected that might have perfected
    The day for one less fortunate.

It wouldn't be possible not to be kind
    In the Land of Beginning Again;
And the ones we misjudged and the ones
      whom we grudged
    Their moments of victory here
Would find in the grasp of our loving handclasp
    More than penitent lips could explain.

For what had been hardest we'd know had been best,
    And what had seemed loss would be gain;
For there isn't a sting that will not take wing
    When we've faced it and laughed it away;
And I think that the laughter is most what we're after
    In the Land of Beginning Again.

So I wish that there were some wonderful place
    Called the Land of Beginning Again,
Where all our mistakes and all our heartaches
    And all of our poor selfish grief
Could be dropped like a shabby old coat at the door,
    And never be put on again.

O TO BE UP AND DOING
ROBERT LOUIS STEVENSON

O to be up and doing,
Unfearing and unashamed to go
In all the uproar and the press
About my human business!
My undissuaded heart I hear
Whisper courage in my ear.

With voiceless calls, the ancient earth
Summons me to a daily birth,
Thou, O my love, ye, O my friends—
The gist of life, the end of ends—
To laugh, to love, to live, to die
Ye call me by the ear and eye!

and the ... be wrong

Sweet Peril
George MacDonald

Alas, how easily things go wrong!
A sigh too much, or a kiss too long,
And there follows a mist and a weeping rain,
And life is never the same again.
Alas, how hardly things go right!
'Tis hard to watch in a summer night,
For the sigh will come, and the kiss will stay,
And the summer night is a wintry day.
And yet how easily things go right,
If the sight and a kiss of a summer's night
Come deep from the soul in the stronger ray
That is born in the light of the winter's day.
And things can never go badly wrong
If the heart be true and the love be strong,
For the mist, if it comes, and the weeping rain
Will be changed by the love into the sunshine again.

Who Has Seen the Wind
Christina Rossetti

Who has seen the wind?
   Neither I nor you:
But when the leaves hang trembling,
   The wind is passing through.

Who has seen the wind?
   Neither you nor I:
But when the trees bow down their heads,
   The wind is passing by.

It Couldn't Be Done
Edgar A. Guest

Somebody said it couldn't be done,
   But he with a chuckle replied
That "maybe it couldn't," but he would be one
   Who wouldn't say so until he had tried.
So he buckled right in with a trace of a grin
   On his face. If he worried he hid it.
He started to sing as he tackled the thing
   That couldn't be done, and he did it.

Somebody scoffed: "Oh, you'll never do that;
   At least no one ever has done it";
But he took off his coat and he took off his hat,
   And the first thing we knew he'd begun it.
With a lift of his chin and a bit of a grin,
   Without any doubting or quiddit,
He started to sing as he tackled the thing
   That couldn't be done, and he did it.

There are thousands to tell you it cannot be done,
   There are thousands to prophesy failure;
There are thousands to point out to you, one by one,
   The dangers that wait to assail you.
But just buckle in with a bit of a grin,
   Just take off your coat and go to it;
Just start to sing as you tackle the thing
   That "cannot be done," and you'll do it.

IN NO STRANGE LAND
FRANCIS THOMPSON

O world invisible, we view thee,
O world intangible, we touch thee,
O world unknowable, we know thee,
Inapprehensible, we clutch thee!

Does the fish soar to find the ocean,
The eagle plunge to find the air—
That we ask of the stars in motion
If they have rumour of thee there?

Not where the wheeling systems darken,
And our benumbed conceiving soars!—
The drift of pinions, would we hearken,
Beats at our own clay-shuttered doors.

The angels keep their ancient places;—
Turn but a stone, and start a wing!
'Tis ye, 'tis your estrangèd faces,
That miss the many-splendoured thing.

But, when so sad thou canst not sadder,
Cry—and upon thy so sore loss
Shall shine the traffic of Jacob's ladder
Pitched betwixt Heaven and Charing Cross.

Yea, in the night, my Soul, my daughter,
Cry—clinging Heaven by the hems;
And lo, Christ walking on the water
Not of Gennesareth, but Thames!

CHARTLESS
EMILY DICKINSON

I never saw a moor,
I never saw the sea;
Yet know I how the
  heather looks,
And what a wave must be.

I never spoke with God,
Nor visited in heaven;
Yet certain am I of the spot
As if the chart were given.

O world unknowable . . .

FROM ODE ON INTIMATIONS OF IMMORTALITY FROM RECOLLECTIONS OF EARLY CHILDHOOD
WILLIAM WORDSWORTH

Our birth is but a sleep and a forgetting:
The Soul that rises with us, our life's Star,
    Hath had elsewhere its setting,
           And cometh from afar:
    Not in entire forgetfulness,
    And not in utter nakedness,
But trailing clouds of glory do we come
    From God, who is our home:
Heaven lies about us in our infancy!
Shades of the prison-house begin to close
    Upon the growing Boy,
But he beholds the light, and whence it flows,
    He sees it in his joy;
The Youth, who daily farther from the east
    Must travel, still is Nature's Priest,
    And by the vision splendid
    Is on his way attended;
At length the Man perceives it die away,
And fade into the light of common day.

THE LAMB
WILLIAM BLAKE

Little lamb, who made thee?
Dost thou know who made thee?
Gave thee life, and bade thee feed
By the stream and o'er the mead;
Gave thee clothing of delight,
Softest clothing, woolly, bright;
Gave thee such a tender voice,
Making all the vales rejoice?
    Little lamb, who made thee?
    Dost thou know who made thee?

    Little lamb, I'll tell thee;
    Little lamb, I'll tell thee:
He is callèd by thy name,
For He calls himself a Lamb.
He is meek, and He is mild,
He became a little child.
I a child and thou a lamb,
We are callèd by His name.
    Little lamb, God bless thee!
    Little lamb, God bless thee!

To a Waterfowl
William Cullen Bryant

Whither, midst falling dew,
While glow the heavens with the last steps of day,
Far, through their rosy depths, dost thou pursue
   Thy solitary way?

Vainly the fowler's eye
Might mark thy distant flight to do thee wrong,
As, darkly seen against the crimson sky,
   Thy figure floats along.

Seek'st thou the plashy brink
Of weedy lake, or marge of river wide,
Or where the rocking billows rise and sink
   On the chafed ocean-side?

There is a Power whose care
Teaches thy way along that pathless coast—
The desert and illimitable air—
   Lone wandering, but not lost.

All day thy wings have fanned,
At that far height, the cold, thin atmosphere,
Yet stoop not, weary, to the welcome land,
   Though the dark night is near.

And soon that toil shall end;
Soon shalt thou find a summer home, and rest,
And scream among thy fellows; reeds shall bend,
   Soon, o'er thy sheltered nest.

Thou'rt gone, the abyss of heaven
Hath swallowed up thy form; yet, on my heart
Deeply has sunk the lesson thou hast given,
   And shall not soon depart.

He who, from zone to zone,
Guides through the boundless sky thy certain flight,
In the long way that I must tread alone,
   Will lead my steps aright.

O rival of the rose . . .

THE RHODORA
RALPH WALDO EMERSON

In May, when sea-winds pierced our solitudes,
I found the fresh Rhodora in the woods,
Spreading its leafless blooms in a damp nook,
To please the desert and the sluggish brook.
The purple petals, fallen in the pool,
Made the black water with their beauty gay;
Here might the red-bird come his plumes to cool,
And court the flower that cheapens his array.
Rhodora! if the sages ask thee why
This charm is wasted on the earth and sky,
Tell them, dear, that if eyes were made for seeing,
Then Beauty is its own excuse for being:
Why thou wert there, O rival of the rose!
I never thought to ask, I never knew:
But, in my simple ignorance, suppose
The self-same Power that brought me there brought you.

TREES
JOYCE KILMER

I think that I shall never see
A poem lovely as a tree.

A tree whose hungry mouth is prest
Against the earth's sweet flowing breast;

A tree that looks at God all day
And lifts her leafy arms to pray;

A tree that may in summer wear
A nest of robins in her hair;

Upon whose bosom snow has lain;
Who intimately lives with rain.

Poems are made by fools like me,
But only God can make a tree.

HIGH FLIGHT
JOHN GILLESPIE MAGEE JR.

Oh! I have slipped the surly bonds of Earth
And danced the skies on laughter-silvered wings;
Sunward I've climbed, and joined
     the tumbling mirth
Of sun-split clouds—and done a hundred things
You have not dreamed of—
     wheeled and soared and swung
High in the sunlit silence. Hov'ring there,
I've chased the shouting wind along, and flung
My eager craft through footless halls of air. . . .

Up, up the long, delirious, burning blue
I've topped the wind-swept heights
     with easy grace,
Where never lark, or even eagle, flew;
And, while with silent,
     lifting mind I've trod
The high untrespassed sanctity of space,
Put out my hand, and touched
     the face of God.

HE HEARS WITH GLADDENED HEART THE THUNDER
ROBERT LOUIS STEVENSON

He hears with gladdened heart the thunder
     Peal, and loves the falling dew;
He knows the earth above and under—
     Sits and is content to view.

He sits beside the dying ember,
     God for hope and man for friend,
Content to see, glad to remember,
     Expectant of the certain end.

I Have Seen a Curious Child
William Wordsworth

  I have seen
A curious child, who dwelt upon a tract
Of inland ground, applying to his ear
The convolutions of a smooth-lipped shell;
To which, in silence hushed, his very soul
Listened intensely; and his countenance soon
Brightened with joy; for from within were heard
Murmurings, whereby the monitor expressed
Mysterious union with its native sea.
Even such a shell the universe itself
Is to the ear of Faith; and there are times,
I doubt not, when to you it doth impart
Authentic tidings of invisible things;
Of ebb and flow, and ever-during power;
And central peace, subsisting at the heart
Of endless agitation.

My Heart's in the Highlands
Robert Burns

My heart's in the Highlands, my heart is not here;
My heart's in the Highlands a-chasing the deer;
Chasing the wild deer, and following the roe,
My heart's in the Highlands, wherever I go.

Farewell to the Highlands, farewell to the North,
The birth-place of valor, the country of worth;
Wherever I wander, wherever I rove,
The hills of the Highlands for ever I love.

Farewell to the mountains, high cover'd with snow;
Farewell to the straths and green valleys below;
Farewell to the forests and wild-hanging woods;
Farewell to the torrents and loud-pouring floods.
My heart's in the Highlands, my heart is not here;
My heart's in the Highlands, a-chasing the deer;
Chasing the wild deer, and following the roe,
My heart's in the Highlands, wherever I go.

I HEAR AMERICA SINGING
WALT WHITMAN

I hear America singing, the varied carols I hear;
Those of mechanics—each one singing his,
   as it should be, blithe and strong;
The carpenter singing his, as he measures his plank or beam,
The mason singing his, as he makes ready for work,
   or leaves off work;
The boatman singing what belongs to him in his boat—
   the deckhand singing on the steamboat deck;
The shoemaker singing as he sits on his bench—
   the hatter singing as he stands;
The wood-cutter's song—the ploughboy's,
   on his way in the morning, or at the noon intermission,
   or at sundown;
The delicious singing of the mother—or of the young wife at work—
   or of the girl sewing or washing;
Each singing what belongs to him or her, and to none else;
The day what belongs to the day—at night,
   the party of young fellows, robust, friendly.
Singing, with open mouths, their strong melodious songs.

If—
Rudyard Kipling

If you can keep your head when all about you
Are losing theirs and blaming it on you;
If you can trust yourself when all men doubt you,
But make allowance for their doubting too;
If you can wait and not be tired by waiting,
Or being lied about, don't deal in lies,
Or, being hated, don't give way to hating,
And yet don't look too good, nor talk too wise;

If you can dream—and not make dreams your master,
If you can think—and not make thoughts your aim;
If you can meet with triumph and disaster
And treat those two impostors just the same;
If you can bear to hear the truth you've spoken
Twisted by knaves to make a trap for fools,
Or watch the things you gave your life to, broken,
And stoop and build 'em up with wornout tools;

If you can make one heap of all your winnings
And risk it on one turn of pitch-and-toss,
And lose, and start again at your beginnings
And never breathe a word about your loss;
If you can force your heart and nerve and sinew
To serve your turn long after they are gone,
And so hold on when there is nothing in you
Except the Will which says to them: "Hold on";

If you can talk with crowds and keep your virtue,
Or walk with kings—nor lose the common touch;
If neither foes nor loving friends can hurt you;
If all men count with you, but none too much;
If you can fill the unforgiving minute
With sixty-seconds' worth of distance run—
Yours is the Earth and everything that's in it,
And—which is more—you'll be a Man, my son!

If you can trust yourself

A LOST CHORD
ADELAIDE ANNE PROCTER

Seated one day at the Organ,
I was weary and ill at ease,
And my fingers wandered idly
Over the noisy keys.

I do not know what I was playing,
Or what I was dreaming then;
But I struck one chord of music,
Like the sound of a great Amen.

It flooded the crimson twilight
Like the close of an angel's Psalm,
And it lay on my fevered spirit
With a touch of infinite calm.

It quieted pain and sorrow,
Like love overcoming strife;
It seemed the harmonious echo
From our discordant life.

It linked all perplexèd meanings
Into one perfect peace,
And trembled away into silence,
As if it were loath to cease.

I have sought, but I seek it vainly,
That one lost chord divine,
That came from the soul of the Organ
And entered into mine.

It may be that Death's bright angel
Will speak in that chord again,—
It may be that only in Heaven
I shall hear that grand Amen.

when all men doubt you

THE FOOL'S PRAYER
EDWARD ROWLAND SILL

The royal feast was done; the King
    Sought some new sport to banish care,
And to his jester cried: "Sir Fool,
    Kneel now, and make for us a prayer!"

The jester doffed his cap and bells,
    And stood the mocking court before;
They could not see the bitter smile
    Behind the painted grin he wore.

He bowed his head, and bent his knee
    Upon the monarch's silken stool;
His pleading voice arose: "O Lord,
    Be merciful to me, a fool!

"No pity, Lord, could change the heart
    From red with wrong to white as wool;
The rod must heal the sin: but, Lord,
    Be merciful to me, a fool!

"These clumsy feet, still in the mire,
    Go crushing blossoms without end;
These hard, well-meaning hands we thrust
    Among the heart-strings of a friend.

"Our faults no tenderness should ask,
    The chastening stripes must cleanse them all;
But for our blunders—oh, in shame
    Before the eyes of heaven we fall.

"Earth bears no balsam for mistakes;
    Men crown the knave, and scourge the tool
That did his will; but Thou, O Lord,
    Be merciful to me, a fool!"

The room was hushed, in silence rose
    The King, and sought his gardens cool,
And walked apart, and murmured low,
    "Be merciful to me, a fool!"

There is no music in the world like this.

L'ENVOI
EDWIN ARLINGTON ROBINSON

Now in a thought, now in a shadowed word,
Now in a voice that thrills eternity,
Ever there comes an onward phrase to me
Of some transcendent music I have heard;
No piteous thing by soft hands dulcimered,
No trumpet crash of blood-sick victory,
But a glad strain of some vast harmony
That no brief mortal touch has ever stirred.
There is no music in the world like this,
No character wherewith to set it down,
No kind of instrument to make it sing.
No kind of instrument? Ah, yes, there is;
And after time and place are overthrown,
God's touch will keep its one chord quivering.

BECAUSE I COULD NOT
STOP FOR DEATH
EMILY DICKINSON

Because I could not stop for Death—
He kindly stopped for me—
The Carriage held but just Ourselves—
And Immortality.

We slowly drove—He knew no haste
And I had put away
My labor and my leisure too,
For His Civility—

We passed the School, where Children strove
At Recess—in the Ring—
We passed the Fields of Gazing Grain—
We passed the Setting Sun—

THE WAKING
THEODORE ROETHKE

I wake to sleep, and take my waking slow.
I feel my fate in what I cannot fear.
I learn by going where I have to go.

We think by feeling. What is there to know?
I hear my being dance from ear to ear.
I wake to sleep, and take my waking slow.

Of those so close beside me, which are you?
God bless the Ground! I shall walk softly there,
And learn by going where I have to go.

Light takes the Tree; but who can tell us how?
The lowly worm climbs up a winding stair;
I wake to sleep, and take my waking slow.

Great Nature has another thing to do
To you and me; so take the lively air,
And, lovely, learn by going where to go.

This shaking keeps me steady. I should know.
What falls away is always. And is near.
I wake to sleep, and take my waking slow.
I learn by going where I have to go.

Or rather—He passed Us—
The Dews drew quivering and chill—
For only Gossamer, my Gown—
My Tippet—only Tulle—

We paused before a House that seemed
A Swelling of the Ground—
The Roof was scarcely visible—
The Cornice—in the Ground—

Since then—'tis Centuries—and yet
Feels shorter than the Day
I first surmised the Horses' Heads
Were toward Eternity—

FROM THE HOUND OF HEAVEN
FRANCIS THOMPSON

I fled Him, down the nights and down the days;
   I fled Him, down the arches of the years;
I fled Him, down the labyrinthine ways
   Of my own mind; and in the midst of tears
I hid from Him, and under running laughter.
     Up vistaed hopes I sped;
     And shot, precipitated
    Adown Titanic glooms of chasmèd fears,
From those strong Feet that followed, followed after.
     But with unhurrying chase,
     And unperturbèd pace,
    Deliberate speed, majestic instancy,
     They beat—and a Voice beat
     More instant than the Feet—
   "All things betray thee, who betrayest Me."

    I pleaded, outlaw-wise,
By many a hearted casement, curtained red,
   Trellised with intertwining charities;
(For, though I knew His love Who followèd,
     Yet was I sore adread
Lest, having Him, I must have naught beside);
But, if one little casement parted wide,
   The gust of His approach would clash it to.
Fear wist not to evade, as Love wist to pursue.
Across the margent of the world I fled,
    And troubled the gold gateways of the stars,
    Smiting for shelter on their clangèd bars;
     Fretted to dulcet jars
And silvern chatter the pale ports o' the moon.
I said to dawn, "Be sudden"; to eve, "Be soon;
   With thy young skiey blossoms heap me over
    From this tremendous Lover!
Float thy vague veil about me, lest He see!"

    I tempted all His servitors, but to find
My own betrayal in their constancy,
In faith to Him their fickleness to me,
   Their traitorous trueness, and their loyal deceit.
To all swift things for swiftness did I sue;
   Clung to the whistling mane of every wind.

But whether they swept, smoothly fleet,
   The long savannahs of the blue;
    Or whether, Thunder-driven,
   They clanged his chariot 'thwart a heaven
Plashy with flying lightnings round the spurn
    o' their feet:
   Fear wist not to evade, as Love wist to pursue.
     Still with unhurrying chase,
     And unperturbèd pace,
   Deliberate speed, majestic instancy,
     Came on the following Feet,
     And a Voice above their beat—
  "Naught shelters thee, who wilt not shelter Me."

       * * *

     Now of that long pursuit
     Comes on at hand the bruit;
   That Voice is round me like a bursting sea:
     "And is thy earth so marred,
     Shattered in shard on shard?
   Lo, all things fly thee, for thou flyest Me!
   Strange, piteous, futile thing,
Wherefore should any set thee love apart?
Seeing none but I makes much of naught" (He said)
"And human love needs human meriting:
    How hast thou merited—
Of all man's clotted clay the dingiest clot?
     Alack, thou knowest not
How little worthy of any love thou art!
Whom wilt thou find to love ignoble thee
    Save Me, save only Me?
All which I took from thee, I did but take,
     Not for thy harms,
But just that thou might'st seek it in My arms.
    All which thy child's mistake
Fancies as lost, I have stored for thee at home;
    Rise, clasp My hand, and come!"
     Halts by me that footfall:
     Is my gloom, after all,
    Shade of His hand, outstretched caressingly?
     "Ah, fondest, blindest, weakest,
     I am He Whom thou seekest!
Thou dravest love from thee, who dravest Me."

Evensong
Robert Louis Stevenson

The embers of the day are red
Beyond the murky hill.
The kitchen smokes; the bed
In the darkling house is spread:
The great sky darkens overhead,
And the great woods are shrill.
So far have I been led,
Lord, by Thy will:
So far have I followed, Lord, and wondered still.
The breeze from the embalmed land
Blows sudden towards the shore,
And claps my cottage door.
I hear the signal, Lord—I understand.
The night at Thy command
Comes. I will eat and sleep and will not question more.

Ballad of Trees and the Master
Sidney Lanier

In the woods my Master went,
Clean forspent, forspent.
Into the woods my Master came,
Forspent with love and shame.
But the olives they were not blind to Him,
The little gray leaves were kind to him:
The thorn-tree had a mind to Him
When into the woods He came.

Out of the woods my Master went,
And he was well content.
Out of the woods my Master came,
Content with death and shame.
When Death and Shame would woo Him last,
From under the trees they drew Him last:
'Twas on a tree they slew Him—last
When out of the woods He came.

The embers of the day

To Althea, from Prison
Richard Lovelace

When Love with unconfinèd wings
  Hovers within my gates,
And my divine Althea brings
  To whisper at the grates;
When I lie tangled in her hair
  And fettered to her eye,
The birds that wanton in the air
  Know no such liberty.

Stone walls do not a prison make,
  Nor iron bars a cage;
Minds innocent and quiet take
  That for an hermitage;
If I have freedom in my love
  And in my soul am free,
Angels alone, that soar above,
  Enjoy such liberty.

On His Blindness
John Milton

When I consider how my light is spent
Ere half my days in this dark world and wide,
And that one talent which is death to hide
Lodged with me useless, though my soul more bent

To serve therewith my Maker, and present
My true account, lest he returning chide,
'Doth God exact day-labor, light denied?'
I fondly ask. But Patience, to prevent

That murmur, soon replies, 'God doth not need
Either man's work or his own gifts. Who best
Bear his mild yoke, they serve him best. His state
Is kingly: thousands at his bidding speed,
And post o'er land and ocean without rest;
They also serve who only stand and wait.'

When in Disgrace—
William Shakespeare

When, in disgrace with fortune and men's eyes,
I all alone beweep my outcast state
And trouble deaf heaven with my bootless cries
And look upon myself and curse my fate,
Wishing me like to one more rich in hope,
Featured like him, like him with friends possess'd,
Desiring this man's art and that man's scope,
With what I most enjoy contented least;
Yet in these thoughts myself almost despising,
Haply I think on thee, and then my state,
Like to the lark at break of day arising
From sullen earth, sings hymns at heaven's gate;
  For thy sweet love remember'd such wealth brings
  That then I scorn to change my state with kings.

The Bridge
Henry Wadsworth Longfellow

I stood on the bridge at midnight,
As the clocks were striking the hour,
And the moon rose o'er the city,
Behind the dark church-tower.

I saw her bright reflection
In the waters under me,
Like a golden goblet falling
And sinking into the sea.

And far in the hazy distance
Of that lovely night in June,
The blaze of the flaming furnace
Gleamed redder than the moon.

Among the long, black rafters
The wavering shadows lay,
And the current that came from the ocean
Seemed to lift and bear them away;

As sweeping and eddying through them,
Rose the belated tide,
And, streaming into the moonlight,
The seaweed floated wide.

And like those waters rushing
Among the wooden piers,
A flood of thoughts came o'er me,
That filled my eyes with tears.

How often, oh, how often,
In the days that had gone by,

I had stood on the bridge at midnight
And gazed on that wave and sky!

How often, oh, how often,
I had wished that the ebbing tide
Would bear me away on its bosom
O'er the ocean wild and wide!

For my heart was hot and restless,
And my life was full of care,
And the burden laid upon me
Seemed greater than I could bear.

But now it has fallen from me,
It is buried in the sea;
And only the sorrow of others
Throws its shadow over me.

Yet whenever I cross the river
On its bridge with wooden piers,
Like the odor of brine from the ocean
Come the thought of other years.

And forever and forever,
As long as the river flows,
As long as the heart has passions,
As long as life has woes.

The moon and its broken reflection
And its shadows shall appear,
As the symbol of love in heaven,
And its wavering image here.

The Loom of Time
Author Unknown

Man's life is laid in the loom of time
    To a pattern he does not see,
While the weavers work and the shuttles fly
    Till the dawn of eternity.

Some shuttles are filled with silver threads
    And some with threads of gold,
While often but the darker hues
    Are all that they may hold.

But the weaver watches with skillful eye
    Each shuttle fly to and fro,
And sees the pattern so deftly wrought
    As the loom moves sure and slow.

God surely planned the pattern:
    Each thread, the dark and fair,
Is chosen by His master skill
    And placed in the web with care.

He only knows its beauty,
    And guides the shuttles which hold
The threads so unattractive,
    As well as the threads of gold.

Not till each loom is silent,
    And the shuttles cease to fly,
Shall God reveal the pattern
    And explain the reason why

The dark threads were as needful
    In the weaver's skillful hand
As the threads of gold and silver
    For the pattern which He planned.

Abou Ben Adhem
James Henry Leigh Hunt

Abou Ben Adhem (may his tribe increase!)
Awoke one night from a deep dream of peace,
And saw, within the moonlight in his room,
Making it rich, and like a lily in bloom,
An Angel writing in a book of gold:
Exceeding peace had made Ben Adhem bold,
And to the Presence in the room he said,
"What writest thou?" The Vision raised its head,
And with a look made of all sweet accord
Answered, "The names of those who love the Lord."
"And is mine one?" said Abou. "Nay, not so,"
Replied the Angel. Abou spoke more low,
But cheerily still; and said, "I pray thee, then,
Write me as one that loves his fellow men."

The Angel wrote, and vanished. The next night
It came again with a great wakening light,
And showed the names whom love of God had blessed,
And, lo! Ben Adhem's name led all the rest!

Huswifery
Edward Taylor

Make me, O Lord, thy spinning wheel complete.
    Thy Holy Word my distaff make for me.
Make mine affections thy swift fliers neate,
    And make my soul thy holy spool to be.
    My conversation make to be thy reel
    And reel the yarn thereon spun of thy wheel.

Then clothe therewith mine understanding, will,
    Affections, judgment, conscience, memory,
My words and actions, that their shine may fill
    My ways with glory and thee glorify.
    Then mine apparel shall display before ye
    That I am clothed in holy robes for glory.

A Psalm of Life
Henry Wadsworth Longfellow

Tell me not, in mournful numbers,
Life is but an empty dream!—
For the soul is dead that slumbers,
And things are not what they seem.

Life is real! Life is earnest!
And the grave is not its goal;
Dust thou art, to dust returnest,
Was not spoken of the soul.

Not enjoyment, and not sorrow
Is our destined end or way;
But to act, that each tomorrow
Find us farther than today.

Art is long, and Time is fleeting,
And our hearts, though stout and brave,
Still, like muffled drums, are beating
Funeral marches to the grave.

Trust no Future, howe'er pleasant!
Let the dead Past bury its dead!
Act,—act in the living Present!
Heart within, and God o'erhead!

Lives of great men all remind us
We can make our lives sublime,
And, departing, leave behind us
Footprints on the sand of time—

Footprints, that perhaps another,
Sailing o'er life's solemn main,
A forlorn and shipwrecked brother,
Seeing, shall take heart again.

Let us, then, be up and doing,
With a heart for any fate;
Still achieving, still pursuing,
Learn to labor and to wait.

All Through the Night
Author Unknown

Sleep, my love, and peace attend thee,
    All through the night;
Guardian angels God will lend thee,
    All through the night;
Soft the drowsy hours are creeping,
Hill and dale in slumber steeping,
Love alone his watch is keeping—
All through the night.

Hark! a solemn bell is ringing,
    Clear through the night;
Thou, my love, art heavenward winging,
    Home through the night;
Earthly dust from off thee shaken,
Soul immortal thou shalt waken,
With thy last dim journey taken
    Home through the night.

Composed upon Westminster Bridge
William Wordsworth

Earth has not anything to show more fair:
Dull would he be of soul who could pass by
A sight so touching in its majesty:
This City now doth, like a garment, wear
The beauty of the morning; silent, bare,
Ships, towers, domes, theatres, and temples lie
Open unto the fields, and to the sky;
All bright and glittering in the smokeless air.
Never did sun more beautifully steep
In his first splendour, valley, rock, or hill;
Ne'er saw I, never felt, a calm so deep!
The river glideth at his own sweet will:
Dear God! the very houses seem asleep;
And all that mighty heart is lying still!

THE TAPESTRY WEAVER
ANSON G. CHESTER

Let us take to our heart a lesson, no braver lesson can be,
From the ways of the tapestry weavers, on the other side of the sea.
Above their head the pattern hangs, they study it with care,
And as to and fro the shuttle leaps their eyes are fastened there.
They tell this curious thing besides, of the patient, plodding weaver;
He works on the wrong side evermore, but works for the right side ever.
It is only when the weaving stops, and the web is loosed and turned,
That he sees his real handiwork, that his marvelous skill is learned.
Ah, the sight of its delicate beauty! It pays him for all its cost.
No rarer, daintier work than his was ever done by the frost!
Then the Master bringeth him golden hire and giveth him praise as well,
And how happy the heart of the weaver is, no tongue but his can tell.

The years of man are the looms of God, let down from the place of the sun,
Wherein we all are weaving, till the mystic web is done,
Weaving blindly but weaving surely, each for himself his fate;
We may not see how the right side looks, we can only weave and wait.
But, looking above for the pattern, no weaver hath need to fear;
Only let him look clear into Heaven—the perfect Pattern is there.
If he keeps the face of the Saviour forever and always in sight,
His toil shall be sweeter than honey, and his weaving is sure to be right.
And when his task is ended, and the web is turned and shown,
He shall hear the voice of the Master; it shall say to him, "Well done!"
And the white-winged angels of heaven, to bear him thence shall come down,
And God shall give him gold for his hire—not coin, but a crown!

the wings of Night . . .

THE DAY IS DONE
HENRY WADSWORTH LONGFELLOW

The day is done, and the darkness
Falls from the wings of Night,
As a feather is wafted downward
From an eagle in his flight.

I see the lights of the village
Gleam through the rain and the mist,
And a feeling of sadness comes o'er me
That my soul cannot resist:

A feeling of sadness and longing,
That is not akin to pain,
And resembles sorrow only
As the mist resembles the rain.

Come, read to me some poem,
Some simple and heartfelt lay,
That shall soothe this restless feeling,
And banish the thoughts of the day.

Not from the grand old masters,
Not from the bards sublime,
Whose distant footsteps echo
Through the corridors of Time.

For, like strains of martial music,
Their mighty thoughts suggest

Life's endless toil and endeavor;
And tonight I long for rest.

Read from some humbler poet,
Whose songs gushed from his heart,
As showers from the clouds of summer,
Or tears from the eyelids start:

Who, through long days of labor,
And nights devoid of ease,
Still heard in his soul the music
Of wonderful melodies.

Such songs have power to quiet
The restless pulse of care,
And come like the benediction
That follows after prayer.

Then read from the treasured volume
The poem of thy choice,
And lend to the rhyme of the poet
The beauty of thy voice.

And the night shall be filled with music,
And the cares, that infest the day,
Shall fold their tents, like Arabs,
And as silently steal away.

About the Poets . . .

No information was available for those poets not listed.

Alford, Henry (1810–1871) English clergyman, scholar, and editor, educated at Cambridge. Served as dean of Canterbury from 1857 to 1871.

Allen, Elizabeth Akers (1832–1911) American poet born in Strong, Maine. Wrote under pseudonym Florence Percy.

Arnold, Matthew (1822–1888) English poet and critic, educated at Balliol at Oxford. Later became poetry professor at Oxford and lectured in the United States.

Babcock, Maltbie Davenport (1858–1901)

Bangs, John Kendrick (1862–1922) American humorist born in Yonkers, New York.

Blake, William (1757–1827) English poet and artist. Worked as an engraver and developed new copper printing process.

Bradstreet, Anne (1612?–1672) Born in England; came to America in 1630. First woman poet to write in English in the American colonies.

Browning, Elizabeth Barrett (1806–1861) English poet born in London. Married poet Robert Browning in 1846 and lived in Italy for several years.

Browning, Robert (1812–1889) English author, playwright, and poet, also wrote psychological monologues. Married poet Elizabeth Barrett in 1846.

Bryant, William Cullen (1794–1878) American poet and editor born in Cummington, Massachusetts, and educated at Williams College. Practiced law before becoming a writer. Co-owner of the New York *Evening Post*.

Robert Burns (1759–1796) Scottish farmer-poet born in Alloway, Scotland. Awarded title National Poet of Scotland.

Byron, George Gordon, Lord (1788–1824) English poet born in London. Penned satires and epic poems.

Carroll, Lewis (1832–1898) Pseudonym of Charles Lutwidge Dodgson, English mathematician and writer. Educated at Rugby and Oxford. Known for his classic children's stories.

Cary, Phoebe (1824–1871) American poet born near Cincinnati, Ohio. Sister of poet Alice Cary.

Clough, Arthur Hugh (1819–1861) English poet born in Liverpool, England. Spent childhood in Charleston, South Carolina, and educated at Oxford.

Coleridge, Samuel Taylor (1772–1834) English poet and critic born in Devonshire, England. Began but did not complete education at Jesus College, Cambridge. Became close friends with Wordsworth.

Coolidge, Susan (1835–1905) Pseudonym of Sarah Chauncey Woolsey. Known for stories for girls.

Craik, Dinah Maria Mulock (1826–1887) English poet, essayist, and novelist born in Staffordshire, England, of Irish extraction.

Dickinson, Emily (1830–1886) American poet born in Amherst, Massachusetts. Composed in solitude most of her life.

Donne, John (1573–1631) English metaphysical poet born in London and educated at Oxford and Cambridge.

Driscoll, Louise (1875–?)

Emerson, Ralph Waldo (1803–1882) American essayist and transcendentalist poet born in Boston, Massachusetts, and educated at Harvard. Worked in the ministry for several years.

Field, Eugene (1850–1895) American poet and journalist born in St. Louis, Missouri, and educated at Williams College. Best known for children's verse.

Foss, Sam Walter (1858–1911) American editor, humorist, and poet of light verse, born in Candia, New Hampshire. Educated at Brown.

Frost, Robert (1874–1963) American poet born in San Francisco and educated at Harvard and Dartmouth. Served as professor of English at Amherst and of poetry at Harvard. Won Pulitzer prizes in 1923, 1930, 1936, and 1942.

Garland, Hamlin (1860–1940) American writer born in West Salem, Wisconsin. Awarded Pulitzer prize in 1921 for *A Daughter of the Middle Border.*

Guest, Edgar A. (1881–1959) Poet born in Birmingham, England; moved to United States at age ten. Humor and verse columnist for *Detroit Free Press.*

Guiterman, Arthur (1871–1943) American poet born in Vienna, Austria. Contributed light verse to numerous periodicals.

Hemans, Felicia D. (1793–1835) English poet born in Liverpool, England. Best known for lyric verse.

Herrick, Robert (1591–1674) English lyric poet. Educated at St. John's, Cambridge. Worked in London as goldsmith and Episcopal minister. Exiled from the ministry due to Royalist sympathies.

Holland, Josiah Gilbert (1819–1881) American writer and editor. Sometimes used pseudonym Timothy Titcomb.

Holmes, Oliver Wendell (1809–1894) American poet, novelist, and essayist born in Cambridge, Massachusetts. Received M.D. degree from Harvard; served as professor of anatomy at Harvard and Dartmouth.

Hood, Thomas (1799–1845) English poet and humorist born in London. Gained popularity through caricatures of current events.

Hopkins, Gerard Manley (1844–1889) English poet. Pioneered poetry innovations such as sprung rhythm and outrides.

Housman, A. E. (1859–1936) English classical scholar and poet, educated at Oxford. Served as professor of Latin at University College in London and Cambridge University.

Howitt, Mary (Botham) (1799–1888) Writer born in England. Co-authored several books with husband, Alfred William Howitt.

Hughes, Langston (1902–1967) American poet, writer, and lecturer born in Joplin, Missouri. Educated at Columbia University and Lincoln University. Awarded a Guggenheim Fellowship in 1935, a Rosewald Fellowship in 1940, and an American Academy of Arts and Letters grant in 1947.

Hunt, James Henry Leigh (1784–1859) English editor, essayist, and poet. Once imprisoned for political works.

Jackson, Helen Hunt (1830–1885) American poet and writer born in Amherst, Massachusetts.

Keats, John (1795–1821) English poet born in London. Received medical degree from Surgeon Guy's Hospital but never practiced.

Kilmer, (Alfred) Joyce (1886–1918) American poet born in New Brunswick, New Jersey. Killed in action during World War I.

Kipling, Rudyard (1865–1936) English writer and poet born in Bombay, India. Educated at United Services College in North Devon, England. Awarded Nobel prize for literature in 1907.

Lanier, Sidney (1842–1881) American poet and musician born in Macon, Georgia. Served in Confederate Army; lectured on English literature at Johns Hopkins University.

Lear, Edward (1812–1888) English landscape painter and poet of nonsense verse.

Longfellow, Henry Wadsworth (1807–1882) American poet born in Portland, Maine, and

educated at Bowdoin. Professor of modern languages at Bowdoin and Harvard. Published more than fourteen volumes of poetry.

Lovelace, Richard (1618–1658) English lyric poet and political writer, educated at Charterhouse School and at Gloucester Hall, Oxford. Imprisoned for his Royalist writings.

Loveman, Robert (1864–1923)

Lowell, James Russell (1819–1891) American poet, essayist, and diplomat born in Cambridge, Massachusetts, and educated at Harvard Law School.

Macdonald, George (1824–1905) Scottish novelist and poet born in Scotland.

Magee, John Gillespie, Jr. (1922–1941) American soldier and poet born in Shanghai. Member of the Royal Canadian Air Force during World War II; killed in an aerial accident over England.

Malloch, Douglas (1877–1938) American poet, writer, and lecturer born in Muskegon, Michigan. Served as president of Chicago Press Club.

Marlowe, Christopher (1564–1593) English dramatist and poet born in Canterbury, England.

Marvell, Andrew (1621–1678) English poet and political satirist.

Masefield, John (1878–1967) English poet, playwright, and fiction writer born in Ledbury, England. Named poet laureate in 1930.

McCrae, John (1872–1918) Canadian physician and poet born in Guelph, Ontario. Lecturer in medicine at McGill medical school. Killed in action during World War I.

Millay, Edna St. Vincent (1892–1950) American author and poet born in Rockland, Maine. Awarded Pulitzer prize for *The Harp Weaver and Other Poems* (1923).

Miller, Joaquin (1841–1913) Pseudonym for Cincinnatus Hiner Miller. American poet

born in Liberty, Indiana. Lived in mining camps in California before studying law.

Milton, John (1608–1674) English poet born in London. Educated at St. John's, Christ's College, Cambridge, and Horton. Continued to write after losing his sight in 1652.

Moore, Rosalie (1910–?)

Moultrie, John (1799–1874) English poet, rector, and hymn writer who fought on side of independence during the American Revolution.

Nash, Ogden (1902–1971) American writer born in Rye, New York. Best known for humorous verse.

Noyes, Alfred (1880–1958) English author and poet born in Staffordshire, England. Professor of modern English literature at Princeton.

Parry, Joseph (1841–1903) Welsh poet and composer; wrote operas, oratorios, cantatas, hymns, and anthems.

Peabody, Josephine Preston (1874–1922) American poet and playwright born in Brooklyn, New York. Won Stratford-upon-Avon prize for her play *The Piper* (1909).

Poe, Edgar Allan (1809–1849) American poet and story writer born in Boston. Dismissed from West Point for disobedience; best known for gothic short works.

Procter, Adelaide Anne (1825–1864) English author and poet; wrote under pseudonym of Mary Berwick.

Riley, James Whitcomb (1849–1916) American poet born in Greenfield, Indiana. Known as the Hoosier Poet and the Poet of Democracy.

Robinson, Corinne Roosevelt (1861–1933) American philanthropist and writer born in New York City and sister of President Theodore Roosevelt. Active in social service during World War I.

Robinson, Edwin Arlington (1869–1935) American poet born in Head Tide, Maine.

Awarded Pulitzer prize in 1921 for *Collected Poems*, in 1924 for *The Man Who Died Twice*, and in 1927 for *Tristram*.

Roethke, Theodore (1908–1963) American poet born in Saginaw, Michigan. Educated at University of Michigan and Harvard. Taught at several colleges, including University of Washington.

Rossetti, Christina Georgina (1830–1894) English poet born in London. Devoted majority of life to religious study.

Sandburg, Carl (1878–1967) American poet and author born in Galesburg, Illinois. Educated at Lombard College; awarded Pulitzer prize for history in 1939 for *Abraham Lincoln—The War Years* and for poetry in 1951 for *Complete Poems*. Awarded Presidential Medal of Freedom in 1964.

Sangster, Margaret E. (1838–1912) American writer and poet. Editor of *Harper's Bazaar* from 1889 to 1899.

Saxe, John Godfrey (1816–1887) American poet born in Highgate, Vermont. Owner and editor of Burlington *Sentinel*; best known for humorous poems.

Scott, Sir Walter (1771–1832) Scottish poet, novelist, historian, and biographer born in Edinburgh, Scotland. Known as the Border Minstrel, the Wizard of the North, and the Great Magician.

Shakespeare, William (1564–1616) English dramatist and poet born in Stratford upon Avon. Composed thirty-five plays, three lyric poems, and more than one hundred sonnets.

Sill, Edward Rowland (1841–1887) American poet and essayist born in Windsor, Connecticut. Educated at Yale; professor of English at University of California.

Stevenson, Robert Louis (1850–1894) Scottish essayist, novelist, and poet born in Edinburgh, Scotland. Moved to America in 1887; lived remaining years on Samoan Islands.

Suckling, Sir John (1609–1642) English Cavalier poet. Credited with inventing game of cribbage.

Taylor, Edward (1674–1729) Born in Leicestershire, England. Served as Puritan minister in American colonies.

Taylor, Jane (1783–1824) English poet born in London. Often collaborated with sister, Ann Taylor.

Teasdale, Sara (1884–1933) American poet born in St. Louis, Missouri. Won Columbia University poetry prize in 1917 for *Love Songs*.

Tennyson, Alfred, Lord (1809–1892) English poet born at Somersby, Lincolnshire. Educated at Cambridge; went on to become poet laureate in 1850.

Thayer, Ernest Lawrence (1863–1940) American lyricist born in Lawrence, Massachusetts.

Thomas, Dylan (1914–1953) English poet born in South Wales.

Thompson, Francis (1859–1907) English poet and literary critic.

van Dyke, Henry (1852–1933) American clergyman, educator, and writer. Professor of English literature at Princeton; U.S. minister to the Netherlands and Luxembourg; and Chaplain in the U.S. Navy.

Wallace, William Ross (1819–1881) American poet and lyricist, penned patriotic verse.

Walter, Howard Arnold (1883–1918)

Whitman, Walt (1819–1892) American poet born in West Hills, Long Island, New York. Worked as schoolteacher, journalist, typesetter, hospital nurse, and clerk.

Whittier, John Greenleaf (1807–1892) American poet born in Haverhill, Massachusetts, and self-educated. Known as "the Quaker Poet."

Wilcox, Ella Wheeler (1850–1919) American journalist and poet born near Madison, Wisconsin. For many years, wrote daily poem for newspaper syndicate.

Wordsworth, William (1770–1850) English poet born in Cockermouth, Cumberland, and educated at Cambridge. Close friends with Coleridge; named poet laureate in 1843.

Work, Henry Clay (1832–1884) American songwriter and poet born in Middletown, Connecticut. Worked as a printer.

Index

Poets

Alford, Henry, 100
Allen, Elizabeth Akers, 63
Arnold, Matthew, 43
Babcock, Maltbie Davenport, 41
Bangs, John Kendrick, 86
Barrington, Patrick, 82
Bennett, John, 100, 107

Titles of Poems

First Lines

Photography Credits

Page 1: Rattlesnake master and prairie blazing star, Iroquois County State Wildlife Area, Illinois. **Pages 2–3**: East branch of Pemigewasset River, White Mountain National Forest, Lincoln, New Hampshire. **6–7**: Union, Kentucky. **9**: Blue violet and grasses, White Mountain National Forest, Woodstock, New Hampshire. **10–11**: Roseshell azaleas, Northeast Harbor, Maine. **13**: Daffodils, Richmond, Virginia. **18–19**: Cannon Ball Mountains and field of lupines, White Mountains, New Hampshire. **21**: Wheat field and views to Adirondack Mountains, Lake Placid, New York. **25**: Willard Brook State Forest, Townsend, Massachusetts. **26–27**: Grayton Beach State Recreation Area, Gulf Coast, Florida. **28–29**: Grand Canyon National Park, Arizona. **Cover and 30–31**: Pemigewasset River, New Hampton, New Hampshire. **32**: Dandelions, McIndoe Falls, Vermont. **34–35**: Meadow grasses, White Mountain National Forest, Livermore, Hew Hampshire. **36–37**: Sugar maple leaves, Ryegate, Vermont. **38–39**: Oaks and sweet birch, Walden Pond, Massachusetts. **40**: Dew-covered spider web. **42–43**: Assateague Island National Seashore, Maryland. **44–45**: Profile Falls, Bristol, New Hampshire. **47**: Joe-pye weed and Connecticut River, Pittsburg, New Hampshire. **48–49**: Shore Acre State Park, Oregon. **51**: Irises, Charlottesville, Virginia. **52–53**: Franconia Range, White Mountain National Forest, Woodstock, New Hampshire. **54–55**: Bass Harbor, Acadia National Park, Mt. Desert Island, Maine. **58–59**: Purple lilacs, Bristol, New Hampshire. **60–61**: Danbury, New Hampshire. **62**: Azaleas, Northeast Harbor, Maine. **67**: Day lilies, Bristol, New Hampshire. **68–69**: Pansies, forsythia, and tulips, Washington, D.C. **70–71**: Red pines and sugar maple saplings, Tamworth, New Hampshire. **72–73**: Grayton Beach State Park, Florida. **74**: Red maples and birches, White Mountain National Forest, New Hampshire. **76–77**: Maples and birches, Waterville Valley, New Hampshire. **79**: Hooksett, New Hampshire. **80–81**: Swift River Valley, White Mountain National Forest, Livermore, New Hampshire. **83**: Robin's plantain and other wildflowers, Bristol, New Hampshire. **84–85**: Sugar maples, New Hampton, New Hampshire. **86**: Old English sheep dog in field. **88–89**: Litchfield, Connecticut. **91**: Red roses, Cape Cod, Massachusetts. **92–93**: Wheat field, Lancaster County, Pennsylvania. **96–97**: Pemigewasset River, New Hampton, New Hampshire. **98–99**: Mt. Washington, Intervale, New Hampshire. **101**: Pasture roses, Franconia, New Hampshire. **103**: Stoney Brook with red maple leaves, Wyman Township, Maine. **104–105**: Daisies and lupines, Plymouth, Hew Hampshire. **108–109**: Field of paintbrush, Independence, Texas. **111**: Oak tree, Bennington County, Vermont. **112–113**: Atchafalaya River, St. Martin Parish, Louisiana. **114–115**: Pemigewasset Valley, White Mountain National Forest, New Hampshire. **116–117**: Oak tree, Bushnell, Florida. **118–119**: Pedernales River, Lyndon B. Johnson Ranch National Historical Park, Texas. **120–121**: Cape Cod, Massachusetts. **122**: Phlox and oak tree, Bushnell, Florida. **124–125**: Pine forest, White Memorial Wildlife Refuge, Litchfield, Connecticut. **126–127**: Spreading lupine and longleaf pine trees, Carolina Sandhills National Wildlife Refuge, South Carolina. **128–129**: Oak tree, Apalachicola State Forest, Fort Gadsden State Park, Florida. **130–131**: Paper birch tree trunks, Grafton Notch State Park, Maine. **133**: Paper birch trees, White Mountain National Forest, Albany, New Hampshire. **134–135**: Hemlock trees, Bristol, New Hampshire. **136–137**: Rio Grande, Big Bend National Park, Texas. **138**: Sherwood red azalea and pine forest, Pine Mountain, Georgia. **140–141**: Bluebonnets, paintbrush, and sotol cactus, Llano County, Texas. **142–143**: Coast Guard Beach, Cape Cod National Seashore, Massachusetts. **144**: Pickens County, South Carolina. **147**: Sugar maples, Bristol, New Hampshire. **148–149**: Contoocook River, Stoddard, New Hampshire. **152–153**: Greens Cliff, White Mountain National Forest, Livermore, New Hampshire.

    All photographs by William Johnson, Johnson's Photography, except for the following: Page 1: Adam Jones Photography. 6–7: Adam Jones Photography. 40: Superstock. 48–49: Dennis Frates, Oregon Scenics. 86: David Stoecklein, The Stock Solution.